CHERYL OBERLE

Folk Vests

25 KNITTING PATTERNS & TALES FROM AROUND THE WORLD

CHERYL OBERLE

Folk Vests

25 KNITTING PATTERNS & TALES FROM AROUND THE WORLD

INTERWEAVE PRESS, INC.
www.interweave.com

Editor: Judith Durant
Technical editor: Dorothy T. Ratigan
Photography: Joe Coca
Illustrations: Gayle Ford
Lino-cuts: Gary Oberle
Cover design: Susan Wasinger
Book design and production: Dean Howes
Proofreaders: Nancy Arndt, Stephen Beal
Indexer: Nancy Arndt
Author photo: Timothy M. Basgall

Interweave Press
201 East Fourth Street
Loveland, Colorado 80537-5655 USA
www.interweave.com

Printed in China through Phoenix Offset

Library of Congress Cataloging-in-Publication Data
    Oberle, Cheryl, 1955-
  Folk vests: 25 knitting patterns and tales from around the world / Cheryl Oberle.
      p. cm.
  Includes bibliographical references and index.
   ISBN 1-931499-14-4
  1. Knitting—Patterns. 2. Vests. I. Title.
  TT835 .O24 2002
  746.43'20432—dc21
                         2002007648

10 9 8 7 6 5 4 3 2 1

This book is dedicated with love and thanks to Gary Oberle and to all the talented folk who create beauty in the everyday world.

Contents

Introduction

A vest is a most versatile garment. It can be worn over or under other clothes; it can be worn opened or closed. It can indicate rank, tell a story, or identify the wearer as a native of a particular land. A vest may be worn for warmth or it may be worn ceremonially. It may be buttoned or laced, layered over other garments, or worn, less demurely, alone. Knitted vests are common garments in many cultures, and vests in all fabrics are found around the world.

Men, women, and children wear vests, often because the vest is so much more comfortable for work and play than is a garment with sleeves. Knitters love to knit vests for the same reason—they are easy to wear and there are no sleeves to knit!

The idea for a book of folk vests came about as I was doing the research for my first book, *Folk Shawls* (Interweave Press, 2000). Nearly every culture that I encountered in my studies had some type of sleeveless garment, and often many styles of such garments.

Vests are so common, in fact, that they are often taken for granted as just something that ``goes under'' a jacket or coat. This ``going under'' is what makes vests so marvelous. Having started out most likely as underwear (a woman's camisole undergarment is still called a vest in England), when vests ``came out'' it was truly a boon to humankind's wardrobe. Often a vest is all we need as an outer garment. A vest also adds just the right amount of extra insulation under a jacket to stop the wind on a blustery day. A vest can carry the symbols and messages that indicate to others how we see ourselves in the world.

The twenty-five vests in this book come from around the world and across time. Their stories and histories are as varied as their styling. The patterns are of varying difficulty and every effort has been made to ensure that the knitter has as good a time knitting them as I had finding and designing them. These are user-friendly patterns. I hope there is a vest here for everyone.

1

1

Scotland

For centuries, rural Scottish women spun and dyed all of the yarn that their families needed for both weaving and knitting. Dyeing handspun yarns with natural dyes produced small amounts of yarn of varying colors and shades. It is thought that woven Scottish plaids may have started as simple checkered patterns used to disguise the many dye lot changes in the weaving yarns. Perhaps the clever Scottish knitters also learned to use small amounts of their naturally dyed yarn in such a manner as to both disguise the dye lots and enhance the patterns.

Crofter's Slipover

Shetland knitters are blessed with a wonderfully wide range of colors in the fleece of the sheep that they raise on their farms or crofts. In shades of white, gray, brown, and black, the natural colors of the sheep allowed knitters to work with a palette that was always harmonious.

The small croft houses had thick stone walls and thatched roofs. Knitting inside was difficult since the only light came from a small oil lamp or through a tiny window. During warm months, knitters often made themselves comfortable by sitting outside on the low stone walls of the house, sheltered from the wind and enjoying the warmth given off by the thatched roof.

Finished Sizes	Chest	Length
Size A	41" (104 cm)	26½" (67.5 cm)
Size B	44½" (113 cm)	27½" (70 cm)
Size C	48" (122 cm)	29½" (75 cm)

Yarn: Jamieson's 2-ply Shetland (100% wool, 150 yd [137 m]/25 g)
Color A (#101 Shetland Black), 2 skeins
Color B (#103 Sholmit), 2 skeins
Color C (#105 Eesit), 2 skeins
Color D (#102 Shaela), 3 skeins
Color E (#104 Natural White), 2 skeins
Color F (#108 Moorit), 1 skein

Needles: 24" (60-cm) circular size 3 (3.25 mm) for A, size 4 (3.5 mm) for B, size 5 (3.75 mm) for C. 16" (40-cm) and 24" (60-cm) circular needles two sizes smaller than needle used for body. Adjust needle size if necessary to obtain the correct gauge.

Notions: Stitch markers; stitch holders

Gauge in Fair Isle pattern on larger needle (see page 128 for two-color swatching instructions)

Size A: 28 sts and 32 rows = 4" (10 cm)
Size B: 26 sts and 30 rows = 4" (10 cm)
Size C: 24 sts and 28 rows = 4" (10 cm)
Remember: Gauge determines how your garment will fit. Swatch until you get it right.

Notes: The slipover is worked circularly up to the shoulders. Steeks are made for the armholes and the neck opening. Work in St st using the two-color stranding technique, carrying the color not in use loosely across the back of the work. Do not carry the yarn over more than 5 sts without catching yarn in the back. See page 128 for techniques.

BOTTOM BORDER

The border is worked in corrugated ribbing. With smaller 24" (60-cm) needle and color A, cast on 288 sts. Being careful not to twist sts, join into a round by knitting into the first st on left needle. This st is the first st of each round. Place a marker at the beginning of the round. This is the left underarm. Work one round of k2, p2 rib in color A.

Work corrugated ribbing in the following color sequence:
Rounds 1–4: K2 A, p2 B
Rounds 5–8: K2 A, p2 C
Round 9–10: K2 D, p2 C
Rounds 11–12: K2 D, p2 E
Rounds 13–14: K2 F, p2 E
Round 15: K2 D, p2 E
Rounds 16–19: K2 D, p2 C
Round 20: K2 A, p2 C
Rounds 21–25: K2 A, p2 B

BEGIN COLOR PATTERN

Next Round: Change to larger needle and begin chart 1. Mark right underarm by placing a marker between the 144th and 145th sts.

Patterns are worked as sets of one XO band, one peerie band, one XO band, and one peerie band.

One pattern set equals 38 rounds. The color sequence for each set is the same. Remember to alternate colors in the steek on every st and every round.

Work in pattern for 2 sets then work rounds 1–18 of the 3rd set, ending 15 sts before left underarm marker.

RESERVE UNDERARM STITCHES

Next Round (round 19 of 3rd set): Place next 29 sts on holder for left underarm. Make a 7-st steek placing a marker on each side of the steek sts; join again by knitting into the next st on left needle. Work to 14 sts before right underarm marker. Place next 29 sts, including marker, on holder.

Make second armhole steek just like the first. Work to end of round.

SHAPE ARMHOLE

Decreases for the armhole shaping are worked on either side of each armhole steek. After 4 decreases, neck shaping begins. Remember to alternate colors on steek sts.

Next Round (round 20 of 3rd set): K1, ssk, knit to 3 sts before first armhole steek, k2tog, k1, knit steek sts, k1, ssk. Knit to last 3 sts before second armhole steek, k2tog, k1. Repeat these decreases every other round 3 more times—228 sts left on needle, including steeks.

Neck shaping begins while armhole decreases are worked 3 more times (7 armhole decrease rounds total).

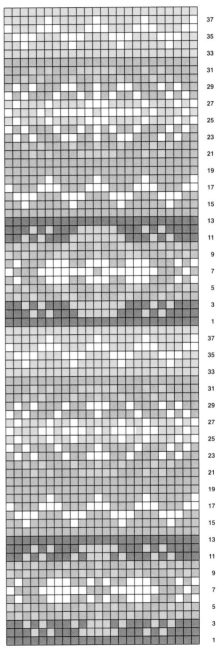

Chart 1 (Sets 1 and 2)

101 Shetland Black (Color A)

103 Sholmit (Color B)

105 Eesit (Color C)

102 Shaela (Color D)

104 Natural White (Color E)

108 Moorit (Color F)

Chart 2 (Sets 3 and 4)

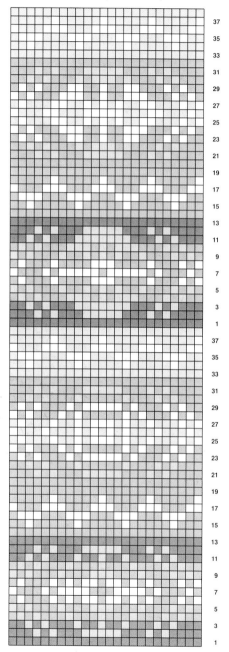

Chart 3 (Set 5)

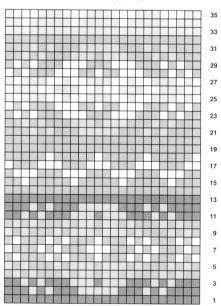

MAKE NECK STEEK

Next Round (round 27 of 3rd set): Work in pattern for 53 sts. Place next st (center stitch of front) on holder. Cast on 7 sts for neck steek. Place markers on each side of steek sts and join to resume circular knitting.

SHAPE NECK

Next Round: Keep the pattern and continue the armhole shaping as established, and at the same time decrease 1 st at each side of the front steek. Work neck decrease round as follows: knit to last 3 sts before front steek, k2tog, k1, knit the steek, k1, ssk.

Repeat this decrease round every other round 2 more times, then every 3rd round 24 times—168 sts on needle.

Continue with pattern as established, ending with round 35 of Set 5. Place all sts on holder.

STITCHING AND CUTTING

Machine stitch and cut steeks for neck and both armholes. See page 129 for steek techniques.

SHOULDERS

Reserve 23 sts for each shoulder, front and back. Bind off shoulders together (see three-needle bind-off on page 127). Keep center 55 back neck sts on holder.

NECKBAND

With smaller 16" (40-cm) needles and color A, begin on right front next to center st and pick up by knitting 66 sts to shoulder, knit 55 back neck sts decreasing 1 st in middle of back neck, 66 sts down front to center st, knit the center st. Place marker on needle, join, and work one round in k2, p2 corrugated ribbing (knit the center st in the same color as the knit sts)—187 sts on needle.

Decrease Round: Work to last 2 sts before the marker, slip 2tog knitwise, remove marker, k1, p2sso, replace marker. Repeat this decrease every round.

Color Sequence:
Round 1: K2 A, p2 A
Round 2: K2 F, p2 E
Rounds 3–4: K2 D, p2 E
Rounds 5–6: K2 D, p2 C
Round 7–8: K2 A, p2 C
Rounds 9–10: K2 A, p2 B
Round 11: K2 A, p2 A

Bind off with A in ribbing.

ARMHOLE BANDS

The armhole bands are worked circularly in corrugated ribbing. With smaller 16" (40-cm) needle and color A, begin at middle of underarm and pick up by knitting 160 sts around armhole including underarm sts. Join and work band color sequence as for neck.

FINISHING

Weave in all ends. Wash and block.

Lichen Waistcoat

One of the most common natural dyes used in Scotland was made from lichen. Easy to use, these plants gave a variety of colors ranging from yellow and gold to the reddish brown that became popular in Harris tweed fabric. The Lichen Waistcoat uses these traditional colors with the same XO and peerie patterns as the Crofter's Slipover. Isn't the difference in appearance amazing?

Yarn: Jamieson's 2-ply Shetland (100% wool, 150 yd [137 m]/25g): Color A (#101 Shetland Black), 5 skeins; Color B (#1190 Burnt Umber), 3 skeins; Color C (#425 Mustard), 2 skeins; Color D (#587 Madder), 1 skein; Color E (#103 Sholmit), 1 skein

Needles: 24" (60-cm) circular size 3 (3.25 mm) for A, size 4 (3.5 mm) for B, size 5 (3.75 mm) for C. 24" (60-cm) and 16" (40-cm) circular needles two sizes smaller than needle used for body. Adjust needle size if necessary to obtain the correct gauge.

Notions: Six ½" (12 mm) buttons; stitch markers; stitch holders

Gauge in Fair Isle pattern on larger needle (see page 128 for two-color swatching instructions)
Size A: 28 sts and 32 rows = 4" (10 cm)
Size B: 26 sts and 30 rows = 4" (10 cm)
Size C: 24 sts and 28 rows = 4" (10 cm)
Remember: Gauge determines how your garment will fit. Swatch until you get it right.

Notes: The waistcoat is worked circularly up to the shoulders. Steeks are made for the front opening and armholes. Work in St st using the two-color stranding technique, carrying color not in use loosely across back of the work. Do not carry the yarn over more than 5 sts without catching yarn in the back. See page 128 for techniques.

BOTTOM BORDER

Border is worked in corrugated ribbing. With smaller

Finished Sizes	Chest	Length
(buttoned, including borders)		
Size A	42¼" (107.5 cm)	24¼" (61.5 cm)
Size B	45½" (115.5 cm)	25½" (65 cm)
Size C	49½" (126 cm)	27" (68.5 cm)

24" (60-cm) needle and color A, cast on 293 sts. Being careful not to twist sts, join into a round by knitting into the first st on left needle. This st is the first st of each round. Place marker at beginning of round and before last 7 sts of round to mark front steek. The last 7 sts of the round are the steek and should be knitted alternating colors on every st and every round (see page 129).

Work corrugated ribbing in the following color sequence:

Rounds 1–3: K2 A, p2 B.
Rounds 4–7: K2 A, p2 C.
Rounds 8–11: K2 A, p2 B.

BEGIN COLOR PATTERN

Next Round: Change to larger needle and knit with Color A, increasing 3 sts evenly spaced—296 sts. Mark underarms by placing a marker between the 72nd and 73rd sts and between the 217th and 218th sts.

Patterns are worked as sets of one XO band and one peerie band. One pattern set equals 19 rounds. The color sequence for each set is the same. Remember to alternate the colors in the steek on every st and every round.

Work in pattern for 4 sets then work rounds 1–18 of the 5th set.

RESERVE UNDERARM STITCHES

Next Round (round 19 of 5th set): Work to 14 sts before right underarm marker. Place next 29 sts, including underarm marker, on a holder. Make a 7-st steek, placing a marker on each side of the steek sts; join again by knitting into the next st on the left needle.

Knit to 15 sts before second marker. Place next 29 sts and underarm marker on a holder. Make second armhole steek just like the first. Place markers on each side of the steek sts, work to end of round.

SHAPE ARMHOLE AND NECK

Decreases for armhole and neck shaping are worked on either side of each respective steek. Remember to alternate colors on the steek sts.

Next Round (round 1 of 6th set): K1, ssk (right neck decrease), knit to 3 sts before right armhole steek, k2tog, k1, knit the steek sts, k1, ssk (right armhole decrease). Knit to 3 sts before left armhole steek, k2tog, k1, knit the steek sts, k1, ssk (left armhole decrease), knit to 3 sts before front steek, k2tog, k1 (left neck decrease). Repeat armhole decreases every other round 8 more times (9 times total). Repeat neck decreases alternating every 3rd and every 4th round 12 more times (13 times total)—164 sts on needle including steeks.

Continue even with pattern as established, completing chart 3. Place all sts on holder.

STITCHING AND CUTTING

Machine stitch and cut the steek for the front opening and both armholes. See pages 128–129 for cutting and steeking techniques.

SHOULDERS

Reserve 23 sts for each shoulder, front and back. Bind off shoulders together (see three-needle bind-off on page 127). Keep center 51 sts on holder for back neck.

FRONT BAND

With smaller needles and Color A, begin at the bottom right front and pick up by knitting 72 sts to beginning of V shaping, 72 sts from point of V to shoulder, knit 51 back neck sts decreasing 1 st in middle of back neck, pick up by knitting 72 sts to beginning of V shaping, and 72 sts down left front to bottom—338 sts on needle). Turn.

Row 1: Purl with A.

Work corrugated ribbing in the following color sequence:

Row 2 (RS): K2 A, p2 B, end k2 A

Row 3: P2 A, k2 B, end p2 A

Row 4: K2 A, p2 B, end k2 A

Row 5: P2 A, k2 C, end p2 A

Buttonholes are worked on 6th and 7th rows of front band.

Row 6 (RS): *K2 A, p2 C for 5 sts, *with color A ssk; with color C (yo) twice; with color A k2tog, work 8 sts in pattern; repeat from * 5 more times, work in pattern to end of row.

Row 7: P2 A, k2 C working k1, p1 into the double yo of the previous row, catching carried strands into the knit st of the k1, p1, end p2A.

Rows 8 and 10: K2 A, p2 C, end k2 A.

Rows 9 and 11: P2 A, k2 B, end p2 A.

Row 12: With A k2, p2, end k2.

With A, bind off loosely in ribbing.

ARMHOLE BANDS

Bands are worked circularly in corrugated ribbing. With smaller 16" (40-cm) needle and color A, begin at middle of underarm and pick up by knitting 156 sts around armhole including underarm sts. Join and knit 1 round. Begin k2, p2 corrugated ribbing in the following color sequence:

Rounds 1–3 and 7–8: K2 A, p2 B

Rounds 4–6: K2 A, p2 C

Round 9: With A, k2, p2

With A, bind off loosely in ribbing.

FINISHING

Weave in all ends. Wash and block.
Sew buttons opposite buttonholes.

■ 101 Shetland Black (Color A)

■ 1190 Burnt Umber (Color B)

□ 425 Mustard (Color C)

■ 587 Madder (Color D)

□ 103 Sholmit (Color E)

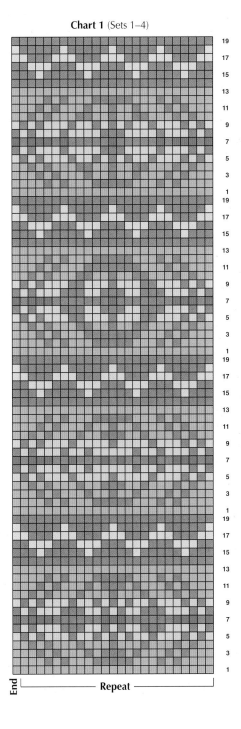

Chart 1 (Sets 1–4)

End ⌐— **Repeat** —⌐

Chart 2 (Sets 5–7)

Chart 3 (Sets 8–10)

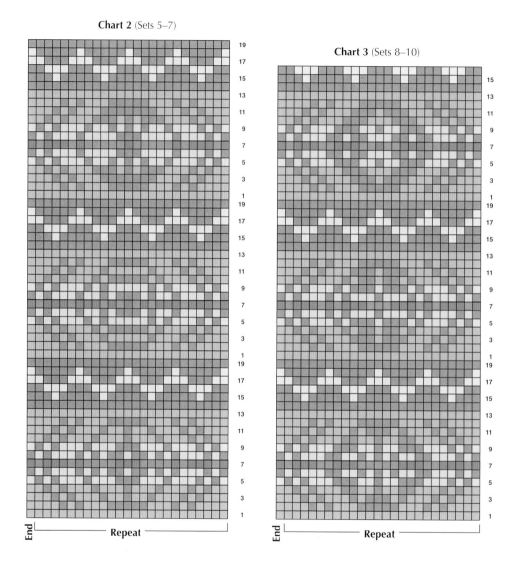

2

Germany

Mother Holle is the heroine of many German legends. A strong fairy woman in her prime, she is a master spinner who was believed by some to have created the world from her spinning wheel. She spends her time in a beautiful garden that has its entrance at the bottom of a wishing well. A lover of human industry, Mother Holle encourages those she comes in contact with to work hard. She especially likes to see a well made bed. Fluffing a German feather bed causes tiny feathers to fly around the room like flakes of snow. During a snow storm it is still common to hear Germans say, "Mother Holle is making her bed."

Clock Vest

Embroidered "clock" patterns have been in use on leg wear in Europe for hundreds of years. Originally used to hide and reinforce the seams at the inner leg and instep of woven hosiery, the designs were later translated into knitting to embellish the more comfortable knitted stockings that became popular in the sixteenth century. Where did clock patterns get their name? While it's origin is still a mystery, the term may have originated to describe the obvious similarity of the designs to the pendulum of a clock.

Finished Sizes   Chest   Length
(buttoned, including borders)

	Chest	Length
Size A	38" (96.5 cm)	18½" (47 cm)
Size B	41½" (105.5 cm)	19½" (49.5 cm)
Size C	46" (117 cm)	21" (53.5 cm)

Yarn: School House Press Québécoise (100% wool, 210 yd [192 m]/3½ oz [100 g]): Deep Red, 3 skeins.

Needles: 24" (60-cm) circular, size 4 (3.5 mm) for A; size 5 (3.75 mm) for B; size 6 (4 mm) for C. 24" (60-cm) and 16" (40-cm) circular needles two sizes smaller than needle used for body. Adjust needle size if necessary to obtain the correct gauge.

Notions: Six ½" (12 mm) buttons, stitch markers, stitch holders, cable needle

Gauge in Stockinette stitch on larger needle
   Size A: 22 sts and 32 rows = 4" (10 cm)
   Size B: 20 sts and 30 rows = 4" (10 cm)
   Size C: 18 sts and 28 rows = 4" (10 cm)

Remember: Gauge determines how your garment will fit. Swatch until you get it right.

BACK AND FRONTS
Back and fronts are worked in one piece to underarm. Read charts from bottom to top and from right to left for right-side rows and from left to right for wrong-side rows.

Using smaller 24" (60-cm) needle, cast on 212 sts. Work rows 1–4 of border chart.

Next Row: Work border chart for 104 sts, work Row 1 of chart C, work border chart to end of row.

Continue working border chart and chart C (chart C will use up border sts on each side as it gets wider) through row 13.

Set-up Row (WS): P19, pm, work set-up row of chart B, pm, p14, pm, work set-up row of chart B, pm,

p42, work chart C as established (row 10), p42, pm, work set-up row chart A, pm, p14, pm, work set-up row of chart A, pm, p19.

Continue working patterns as established through row 59 of chart C.

DIVIDE FOR UNDERARMS/RESERVE UNDERARM AND FRONT STITCHES

Next Row (WS—row 60 of chart C): Work in pattern as established to 2 sts past left-side cable, place last 15 sts worked on holder for left underarm. Work in pattern as established to end of right-side cable and place last 15 sts worked on holder for right underarm. Work to end of row, break off yarn, and place both fronts on holders, leaving only center 90 sts on needle for back.

Next Row (RS): Knit to center 30 sts. Work row 61 of chart C, knit to end of row—91 sts. Turn.

Next Row (WS): Work in established patterns to end, knitting the increased stitch (set-up row for chart D).

BACK

Begin chart D and Shape Armholes

Next Row (RS): K1, ssk (armhole shaping), work in pattern as established to center 31 sts. Work next 13 sts as row 13 of chart B (these 13 sts will be worked as chart B for the rest of the back), work row 1 of chart D (5 sts), work next 13 sts as row 13 of chart A (these 13 sts will be worked as chart A for the rest of the back), work in pattern to last 3 sts, k2 tog, k1 (armhole shaping). Work armhole shaping every other row 6 more times (7 times total)—77 sts on needle.

At the same time:

In order to accommodate the increases in chart D, decreases must be worked on the outside of charts B

and A. Work as follows: knit to one st before chart B, p2tog (one knit st and the first purl st of chart B), work chart B, work chart D as established, work chart A to last purl st, p2tog (the last purl st of chart A and one knit st), knit to end of row. Repeat these decreases every 4th row on same rows as chart D has increases. When the increases of chart D stop (row 63), stop the decreases as well.

Work in pattern as established until chart D is complete. Place back sts on holder. You should end on row 14 of charts A and B.

LEFT FRONT

Place left-front sts on needle. Work 2 rows in established pattern.

Next Row (RS—row 13 of chart B): K1, ssk (armhole shaping), work in pattern as established to end. Repeat armhole shaping every other row 6 more times (7 times total)—39 sts on needle. Work in pattern until 2 full repeats of chart B have been completed from top of border, then work rows 1–30 once more.

Shape Neck

Next Row (RS): Work in pattern to end of row, break yarn. Turn and place first 14 sts on holder. Attach yarn and work (WS) row to end.

Decrease Row (RS): Work in pattern to last 3 sts, k2tog, k1. Work this decrease row every other row 2 more times—22 sts left on needle. Work in pattern until 3 full repeats of chart B have been completed from top of border, then work rows 1–20 once more.

RIGHT FRONT

Place right-front sts on needle. Work 2 rows in established pattern.

Next Row (RS—row 13 of chart A): Work in pattern as established to last 3 sts, k2tog, k1 (armhole shaping). Repeat armhole shaping every other row 6 more times (7 times total)—39 sts on needle. Work in pattern until 2 full repeats of chart A have been completed from top of border, then work rows 1–30 once more.

Shape Neck

Next Row (RS): Work first 14 sts in pattern and place them on holder, work in pattern to end. Turn and work back.

Decrease Row (RS): K1, ssk, work in pattern to end. Work this decrease row every other row 2 more times—22 sts left on needle. Work in pattern until 3 full repeats of chart A have been completed from top of border, then work rows 1–20 once more.

SHOULDERS

With right sides together, bind off shoulders together (see three-needle bind-off on page 127).

FRONT BORDERS

Button band

With smaller 24" (60-cm) needle, pick up by knitting 82 sts along left front edge. Purl one row (WS). Work rows 1–11 of border chart. Bind off loosely in pattern.

Buttonhole Band

With smaller 24" (60-cm) needle, pick up by knitting 82 sts along right front edge. Purl one row (WS). Work border chart through row 4.

Next Row: Work in pattern for 3 sts, *k2tog, (yo) twice, work 13 sts in pattern; repeat from * 4 more times (5 times total) end k2tog, (yo) twice, work 2 sts in pattern.

Next Row: Work in pattern as established working double yarnovers as one stitch (drop extra loop of double yarnover). Continue in pattern through row 11 of border chart. Bind off loosely in pattern.

NECKBAND

With smaller 24" (60-cm) needle and beginning at top of right-front band, pick up by knitting 121 sts around neck edge as follows: pick up 7 sts across top edge of right-front band, 14 sts from right-front neck holder, 23 to shoulder, 33 from back-neck holder, 23 from shoulder to left-front neck holder, 14 from left-front neck holder, and 7 sts across top of left-front band. Turn and knit two rows. Bind off loosely in knit.

ARMHOLE BANDS (worked circularly)

With 16" (40-cm) needle, pick up 124 sts around armhole as follows: Beginning at middle of underarm, place first 8 sts on needle, k2tog, k1, k2tog, k1, k2tog, pick up by knitting 57 st to shoulder, pick up 57 st from shoulder to last 7 sts on underarm holder, place these sts on needle, k1, k2tog, k1, k2tog, k1. Join and knit one round, then work 2 rounds of border pattern. Bind off in pattern.

FINISHING

Weave in all ends. Wash and block.
Sew buttons into place along front edge opposite buttonholes.

□ knit RS; purl on WS

▨ purl on RS; knit on WS

x increase 1 stitch

b knit in back of stitch

2/2 Right Cross: place next 2 sts on cable needle and hold in back, k2b, k2b from cable needle

2/2 Left Cross: place next 2 sts on cable needle and hold in front, k2b, k2b from cable needle

2/2 Purl Right Cross: place next 2 sts on cable needle and hold in back, k2b, p2 from cable needle

2/2 Purl Left Cross: place next 2 sts on cable needle and hold in front, p2, k2b from cable needle

2/1 Right Cross: place next st on cable needle and hold in back, k2b, k1b from cable needle

2/1 Left Cross: place next 2 sts on cable needle and hold in front, k1b, k2b from cable needle

2/1 Purl Right Cross: place next st on cable needle and hold in back, k2b, p1 from cable needle

2/1 Purl left Cross: place next 2 sts on cable needle and hold in front, p1, k2b from cable needle

1/1 Right Cross: place next st on cable needle and hold in back, k1b, k1b from cable needle

1/1 Left Cross: place next st on cable needle and hold in front, k1b, k1b from cable needle

1/1 Purl Right Cross: place next st on cable needle and hold in back, k1b, p1 from cable needle

1/1 Purl Left Cross: place next st on cable needle and hold in front, p1, k1b from cable needle

Border

| End | Repeat |

Chart A

Set-up row

Chart B

Set-up row

18

Chart D

Chart C

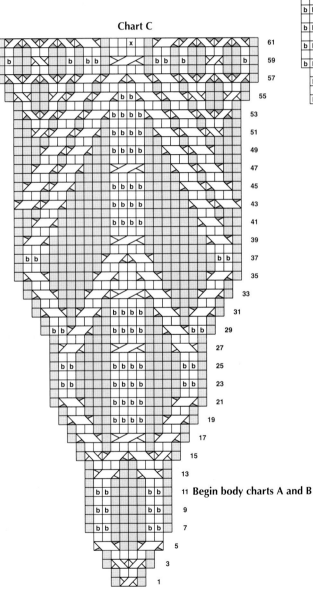

11 **Begin body charts A and B**

Set-up row

Many Buttoned Vest

The Many Buttoned Vest is a modern folk vest. Perfect for button lovers and collectors, it can be used to showcase many favorite buttons. The knitted design is most likely based on the laced-front vests worn with traditional German folk costumes.

While traveling in Europe, a knitter from Texas came across a simple version of this pattern. She purchased yarn and knitted the vest on her journey. As she went she collected buttons from her destinations to embellish the vest. The vest became her favorite souvenir as she placed the buttons (thirty of them) in columns down the front edges. This version has twenty buttons. You may add as many buttons as you'd like. What's even better? No buttonholes!

The Many Buttoned Vest is a simple garter stitch cardigan with cables and I-cord trim.

Finished Sizes	Chest	Length
Size A	41" (104 cm)	22½" (57 cm)
Size B	45½" (115.5 cm)	24½" (62 cm)
Size C	50" (127 cm)	26½" (67.5 cm)

Yarn: Knit One Crochet Too Parfait Solids (100% wool, 218 yd [200 m]/3.5 oz [100 g]): #1730 Eggplant, 4 skeins.

Needles: 24" (60-cm) circular size 7 (4.5 mm). Set of double-pointed needles one size larger than needle used for body. Adjust needle size if necessary to obtain the correct gauge.

Notions: Twenty to thirty ½" to ¾" (12 mm to 19 mm) buttons; backing buttons, same number as buttons; stitch markers; stitch holders; cable needle

Gauge in Garter stitch on larger needle
16 stitches and 30 rows = 4" (10 cm)
Remember: Gauge determines how your vest will fit. Swatch until you get it right.

The vest is worked back and forth in one piece to the underarms. The stitches between cable patterns are worked in garter stitch (knit every row).

With 24" (60-cm) needle, cast on 194 (212, 230) sts.
Set-up row (WS): K14 (15, 16), pm; k2, p4, k2, p2, k1, (row 8 of chart A) pm; k21 (25, 29), pm for underarm, k21 (25, 29), pm; k2, p4, k2, p2, k1, (row 8 of chart A) pm; k7, pm; k2, [p4, k4] twice, p4, k2, (row 16 of chart B) pm; k7, pm; k2, p4, k2, p2, k1, (row 8 of chart A) pm; k21

(25, 29), pm for second underarm, k21 (25, 29), pm; k2, p4, k2, p2, k1, (row 8 of chart A) pm; k14 (15, 16).

Follow charts A and B as established until piece measures 13 (14½, 16)" (33 [37, 40.5] cm), ending with a RS row.

DIVIDE FOR UNDERARMS

Next Row (WS): Work in pattern as established to 4 (8, 12) sts past first underarm marker, place last 8 (16, 24) sts worked (including marker) on holder for left underarm. Work to 4 (8, 12) sts past second underarm marker and place last 8 (16, 24) sts worked (including marker) on holder for right underarm. Work to end of row and place both fronts on holders—94 sts on needle for back.

BACK

Shape Armholes

Next Row (RS): Join new yarn, work in pattern as established, and decrease 1 st at each armhole edge as follows: k1, ssk, work in pattern as established to last 3 sts, k2tog, k1.

Work these decreases every other row 5 more times (6 times total)—82 sts left on needle. Work in pattern until armhole measures 9½ (10, 10½)" (24 [25.5, 26.5] cm) from underarm. Place back sts on holder.

LEFT FRONT

Place 42 (43, 44) left-front stitches on needle.

Next Row (RS): Join yarn and shape armholes as follows: k1, ssk, work in pattern as established to end. Work decreases every other row 5 more times (6 times total)—36 (37, 38) sts left on needle. Work in pattern until armhole measures 6½ (7, 7½)" (16.5 [18, 19] cm) from underarm, ending with a WS row.

Shape Neck

Next Row (RS): Work in pattern to last 9 (10, 11) sts and place them on a holder. Turn and work back.

Decrease Row (RS): Work in pattern to last 3 sts, k2tog, k1. Work decreases every other row 2 more times (3 times total)—24 sts left on needle.

Continue in pattern on remaining sts until front has same number of rows as back. Place left-front sts on holder.

RIGHT FRONT

Place 42 (43, 44) right-front sts on needle.

Next Row (RS): Join yarn. Shape armholes as follows: work in pattern as established to last 3 sts, k2tog, k1. Repeat this shaping every other row 5 more times (6 times total)—36 (37, 38) sts left on needle. Work in pattern until armhole measures 6½ (7, 7½)" (16.5 [18, 19] cm) from the underarm, ending with a WS row.

Shape Neck

Next Row (RS): Work first 9 (10, 11) sts in pattern and place them on a holder, work in pattern to end. Turn and work back.

Decrease Row (RS): K1, ssk, work in pattern to end. Work decreases every other row 2 more times—24 stitches left on needle.

Continue in pattern on remaining sts until front has same number of rows as back. Place right front sts on holder.

SHOULDERS

Bind off shoulders together (see three-needle bind-off on page 127).

Front/Neck Border

With larger double-pointed needle, cast on 3 sts. Knit

3-st I-cord (see page 127) to front edge and neck as follows: begin at bottom of right front and attach to vest between garter ridges; at right neck corner work two rows without attaching to make a square corner; attach to each st from right front neck holder; attach between ridges up to shoulder; attach to each st from back neck holder; attach between ridges down to left-front neck holder; attach to each st from left-front neck holder; at corner work two rows without attaching to make a square corner; attach between ridges down left front to bottom. Cut yarn.

Armhole Borders

Beginning at the middle of the underarm stitches, knit and attach 3-st I-cord to each underarm stitch and between ridges around armhole. Sew ends of I-cord together.

FINISHING

Weave in all ends. Wash and block.

Sew buttons along front edges. (Note: It is a good idea to use the old tailor's trick of sewing on light-weight backing buttons to support the weight of the real buttons.)

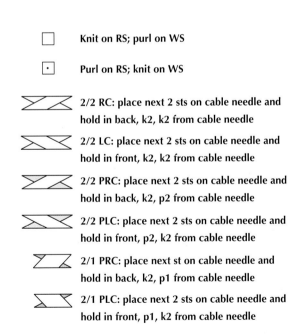

Knit on RS; purl on WS

Purl on RS; knit on WS

2/2 RC: place next 2 sts on cable needle and hold in back, k2, k2 from cable needle

2/2 LC: place next 2 sts on cable needle and hold in front, k2, k2 from cable needle

2/2 PRC: place next 2 sts on cable needle and hold in back, k2, p2 from cable needle

2/2 PLC: place next 2 sts on cable needle and hold in front, p2, k2 from cable needle

2/1 PRC: place next st on cable needle and hold in back, k2, p1 from cable needle

2/1 PLC: place next 2 sts on cable needle and hold in front, p1, k2 from cable needle

Chart A

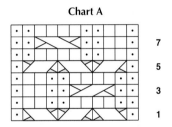

Chart B

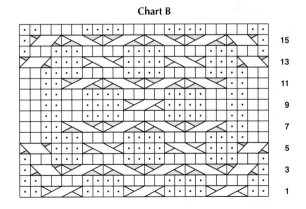

3

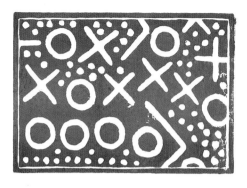

Africa

The Kasai River region of Africa is home to the Bushoong people. Masters of surface design, the Bushoong weave long pieces of cloth from raffia and then embellish them with dyes and embroidery. Using mostly geometric designs, they have over two hundred patterns that are freely combined, and many different designs often appear on the same garment. The cloth is worn by men and women as a skirt, or mapel, wrapped many times around the body and then draped over the shoulder. Some men's mapels are over nine yards in length.

Kasai Vest

The pattern design of the Kasai Vest was inspired by a woman's ceremonial skirt from the Cotsen Collection in the Museum of International Folk Art in Santa Fe, New Mexico.

Finished Sizes	Chest	Length
Size A	41½" (105.5 cm)	19¾" (50 cm)
Size B	44½" (113 cm)	21" (53.5 cm)
Size C	47½" (120.5 cm)	22½" (57 cm)

Yarn: Jamieson and Smith's 2-ply Shetland (100% wool, 150 yd [137 m]/25 g): #81 Charcoal (Color A) 6 skeins; #FC45 Tan (Color B) 3 skeins.

Needles: 24" (60-cm) circular size 3 (3.25 mm) for A, size 4 (3.5 mm) for B, size 5 (3.75 mm) for C. 24" (60-cm) and 16" (40-cm) circular needles one size smaller than needle used for body. Adjust needle size if necessary to obtain the correct gauge.

Notions: One 1⅜" (35 mm) button; stitch markers; stitch holders

Gauge in two-color pattern using chart 1 on larger
    needle
    Size A: 28 sts and 34 rows = 4" (10 cm)
    Size B: 26 sts and 32 rows = 4" (10 cm)
    Size C: 24 sts and 30 rows = 4" (10 cm)
    Remember: Gauge determines how your garment
will fit. Swatch until you get it right.

Note: The front band of the Kasai Vest shapes the garment by being shorter than the front opening as knitted.

Except for the bottom border facing, the vest is worked
circularly up to the shoulders. Steeks are made for the
front opening and the armholes. Work in St st using the
two-color stranding technique, carrying the color not
in use loosely across the back of the work. Do not carry
the yarn over more than 5 sts without catching yarn in
the back. (See page 128–129 for stranding and steek
techniques.)

BOTTOM BORDER AND FACING

The border is worked in St st with a facing. The facing
is worked flat and after the facing is complete the sts
will be joined to begin circular knitting.

With smaller 24" (60-cm) needle, color A, and using
a provisional cast on (see page 124), cast on 250 sts.

Work 10 rows of St st (knit one row, purl one row)
ending with a purl row.

Folding Ridge
Change to larger 24" (60-cm) needle and purl the next
(RS) row. Do not turn.

STEEK AND JOIN

Cast on 7 sts on right needle using the backward loop
method (see page 124). Place a marker on each side of
the steek sts. Join, being sure that your sts are not twisted, by knitting into the first st on the left needle. This st
is the first st of each round.

Knit the first round, marking the sides by placing a
marker between the 53rd and 54th sts and between
the 197th and 198th sts—257 sts on needle.

MAIN COLOR PATTERN

Work rounds 1–31 of chart 1 once.

Begin chart 2 and work rounds 1–51. Remember
to alternate the colors in the steek on every st and
every round.

RESERVE UNDERARM STITCHES

Next Round (round 52 of chart 2): Work to 15 sts
    before right underarm marker. Place next 30 sts,
    including marker, on holder.

MAKE ARMHOLE STEEKS

Cast on 7 sts on right needle using the backward
loop method. Place a marker on each side of the
steek sts. Join by knitting into the next st on left
needle.

Knit to 15 sts before left underarm marker. Place next 30 sts, including marker, on holder.

Make the second armhole steek just like the first, placing markers on each side of the steek sts.

Knit to end of round—211 sts on needle including steeks.

SHAPE ARMHOLE

Decreases for armhole shaping are worked on either side of each armhole steek. Remember to alternate the colors on the steek sts.

Keeping pattern as established, work armhole decreases as follows: Knit to 3 sts before right armhole steek, k2tog, k1, knit the steek sts, k1, ssk. Knit to 3 sts before left armhole steek, k2tog, k1, knit the steek sts, k1, ssk, knit to end of round. Repeat these decreases every other round 7 more times (8 times total)—179 left on needle, including steeks. Work in established pattern through round 73, then work rounds 1–55 once more. Put all sts on holder.

STITCHING AND CUTTING

Machine stitch and cut steeks for front opening and armholes (see page 129).

SHOULDERS

Reserve 30 sts for each shoulder, front and back. Bind off the shoulders together (see three-needle bind-off on page 127). Keep center 38 sts on holder for back neck.

FRONT/NECKBAND

Note: In order for the band to shape the vest, fewer stitches than normal are picked up along the front edges. If a straight vest is desired, use the numbers in parentheses for the front band. Instructions are given for knitting the band flat (back and forth) or circularly.

Flat Version
With the larger 24" (60-cm) needle and color A, begin

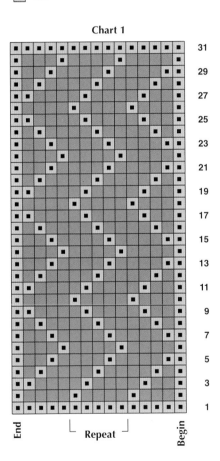

Charcoal

Tan

Chart 1

31 29 27 25 23 21 19 17 15 13 11 9 7 5 3 1

End Repeat Begin

Chart 2

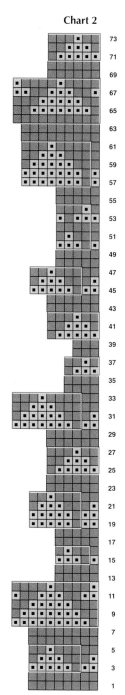

**Begin as indicated; repeat highlighted box
(end wherever you are in the pattern)**

at the bottom of right front and pick up by knitting 108 (123) sts along the right-front edge. Knit 38 back neck sts, increasing 1 st in center of back neck, and pick up by knitting 108 (123) sts down left-front edge—255 (285) sts on needle. Work Rows 1–22 of chart 1. With color B, knit one row. With color A, purl one row.

Facing
Next Row: With color A, purl one (RS) row (folding ridge). Turn, and beginning with a purl row, work St st in the following stripe sequence:
9 rows color A
2 rows color B
4 rows color A
1 row color B
4 rows color A
2 rows color B
7 rows color A
  Place all sts on holder. Tack down live sts to inside, covering cut edge.

Circular Version
Set up for circular knitting as follows: At the end of the pick-up row, place marker on needle, cast on 8 sts for steek, place another marker on needle, join to beginning of the pick-up round, making sure band sts are not twisted.
  Work rounds 1–22 of chart 1 as a circular chart (read all rows from right to left). With color B, knit one round; with color A, knit one round.

Facing
The facing is knitted back and forth, not circularly. Turn and with color A, knit one (WS) row (folding ridge). Turn, and beginning with a knit row, work St st in the same stripe sequence as for flat version. Place all sts on holder.
  Cut through the steek sts. (Machine stitch before cutting if necessary; see page 129). Tack down live sts

to inside, covering cut edge. Fold extra sts up into the inside of the border and tack end of border closed.

ARMHOLE BORDERS

Armhole borders are worked circularly in St st with a facing.

With 16" (40-cm) circular needle and beginning at middle of underarm holder, pick up by knitting 130 sts around the armhole including underarm sts. Join and knit 1 round. Purl the next round for the folding ridge. Knit 7 more rounds and place sts on holder. Turn armhole facing to WS at purl row. Tack down live sts to inside, covering cut edge.

FINISHING

Bottom Facing
Remove provisional cast-on and tack down live sts to inside. Weave in all ends. Wash and block.

Button and Button Loop
Make a loop from twisted cord with color A (see page 127). For the best fit, try on vest, cross fronts right over left, and mark the spot for button. Sew on the button and then pin and sew the button loop at the appropriate place on the inside of right-front facing (not through both layers).

4

Nepal

Nepal, whose name is thought to have come from the Sanskrit word for "home," was largely isolated from the modern world until the 1970s. Country folk live a simple life based on the traditions and beliefs of their ancestors. Striped fabrics and vibrant colors abound in the clothing of the Nepalese, who are descended from many ancient tribes and races.

Sari Silk Vest

Spinners in Nepal use a primitive, often hand-made, spinning wheel called a charka. Charkas are treasured possessions because a spinner can sell her yarn to supplement the meager livelihood produced by farming. Some charkas are so beautifully carved that they have become collectors' pieces in the west. Yarn is spun from wool and sometimes from the remnants of silk fabric that is woven in India and used to make saris and other clothing. The Sari Silk Vest is knitted with this unique handspun recycled silk yarn.

Finished Sizes	Chest	Length
Size A	38" (96.5 cm)	23" (58.5 cm)
Size B	42" (106.5 cm)	24" (61 cm)
Size C	46" (117 cm)	25" (63.5 cm)

Yarn: Himalaya Yarn Recycled Silk handspun yarn (100% silk, 100 yd [91 m]/100 g): 3 different skeins in jewel tones (Color A). Himalaya Yarn 100% Silk handspun yarn (100% silk, 180 yd [165 m]/100 g): 2 skeins Amethyst (Color B).

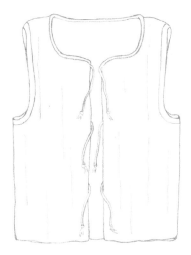

Needles: 24" (60-cm) circular size 10 (6 mm). Crochet hook size H.

Gauge in pattern
  10½ sts and 20 rows = 4" (10 cm)
  Remember: Gauge determines how your garment will fit. Swatch until you get it right.

Notes: Because of its open stitch pattern, the Sari Silk vest is a very flexible garment that looks compact but accommodates a wide range of sizes. The vest can be worn in a variety of ways. It can be tied in front with the optional ties; the ties can be woven into the fabric so that they disappear and the vest can be worn open; the open vest can be crossed in front and pinned or buttoned at the waist for a more tailored look.

Larger sizes can be achieved by simply adding a repeat of the pattern rows at each underarm. Each ten pattern rows (one repeat) equals two inches, so two patterns will add four inches to the garment. Just remember to work one repeat on each side or you'll get a very strange garment. If you would prefer to add width to the back and fronts instead of the sides, you may add eight inches by adding two repeats on the

back and one on each front. There are many different combinations that will work here. If you only need to add four inches but want those inches on the back and front, not on the sides, then follow the instructions for the medium size garment but add two repeats on the back and one repeat on each front. Since the medium is already four inches smaller than the large, adding eight inches to it will make it the same size as the large plus four inches (two repeats) with the extra fabric on the back and front instead of on the sides. Be careful, though; remember that whether we gain or lose weight the width of our shoulders is one measurement that doesn't change (at least there's one). Adding repeats to the fronts and backs will make the armhole drop over the shoulder more; adding repeats at the sides adds width only to the body, not the shoulder. Remember too, to purchase more yarn if you intend to enlarge the garment; buy at least one more ball of each color.

The vest is knitted side to side from the right-front edge to the left-front edge. The armhole and neck have single-crochet trim. Optional ties are attached to the front edge.

Change from one color A skein to another on row 7 of the pattern st. This will blend all the colors and textures of the recycled yarn to give the most pleasing effect.

You will be changing yarns frequently. Do not carry yarns along edges; cut them when changing colors, leaving a tail.

PATTERN STITCH
Rows 1 and 2: With color A, knit.
Rows 3–6: With color B, knit.
Rows 7 and 8: With color A, knit.
Row 9: With color A, knit, wrapping yarn 3 times around needle on each st.
Row 10: With color A, knit, dropping extra loops on each st.
  Repeat rows 1–10 for pattern.

RIGHT SIDE

Set Up/Front Border

With 24" (60-cm) needle and color B, cast on 51 (54, 57) sts. Knit 4 rows. Begin pattern st on row 7 and work through row 10. Mark this row.

Work until one whole repeat of rows 1–10 (counting from marker) is complete. Work rows 1 and 2 of the second repeat.

SHAPE NECK

At end of row 3 of second repeat, cast on 9 sts. Continue in pattern through 3rd repeat. Work rows 1–5 of 4th repeat.

SHAPE ARMHOLE

On row 6 of 4th repeat, bind off first 24 (27, 27) sts. Work in pattern to end. Continue in pattern st until 4 (5, 6) repeats have been completed. Work rows 1 and 2 of the 5th (6th, 7th) repeat. At end of row 3 of 5th (6th, 7th) repeat, cast on 24 (27, 27) sts (armhole shaping complete).

Continue in pattern st until 12 (13, 14) repeats have been completed. Work rows 1–5 of 13th (14th, 15th) repeat (back completed).

SHAPE ARMHOLE

On row 6 of 13th (14th, 15th) repeat, bind off first 24 (27, 27) sts. Work in pattern to end. Continue in pattern st until 13 (15, 17) repeats have been completed. Work Rows 1 and 2 of 14th (16th, 18th) repeat. At end of row 3 of 14th (16th, 18th) repeat, cast on 24 (27, 27) sts (armhole shaping complete).

SHAPE NECK

At beginning of row 6 of 16th (18th, 20th) repeat, bind off 9 sts. Continue in pattern through 18th (20th, 22nd) repeat. Work rows 1–6 once more.

FRONT BORDER

With color B knit 2 rows. Bind off loosely.

SHOULDERS

With right sides held together, sew fronts to back at shoulders.

NECK BORDERS

With crochet hook and color B, work one row of single crochet (see below), working 2 sts and skipping 1 around neck edge.

ARMHOLE BORDERS

With crochet hook and color B, work one round of single crochet, working 2 sts and skipping 1 around armhole edge.

FINISHING

Front Ties

Make 6 twisted cord ties (see page 127). Start with one yard of color B for each tie.

Weave in all ends. Wash and block.
Attach ties where desired on front.

SINGLE CROCHET EDGING

With right side facing and slip knot on hook, *insert hook into stitch, yarn over hook and draw a loop through stitch, yarn over hook (figure 1) and draw a loop through both loops on hook (figure 2). Repeat from *. Join to beginning with a slip stitch. **Figure 1**

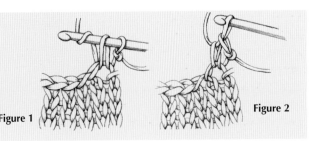

Figure 2

5

Ireland

Irish knitters have taken the simple common cable and turned it into a wonderful library of designs. In modern times romantic stories of the origins and meaning of these patterns have become popular, and if the patterns did not originally have any particular symbolism, they certainly have it for knitters now.

Expert spinner Rachel Brown of Taos, New Mexico, suggested a theory for the origin of the use of cabled patterns in knitting: Much of the handspun yarn in earlier days was a single-ply yarn that, when knitted, tended to create a biased fabric. Lots of cable crossings will control the yarn and so will keep the knitted fabric from becoming distorted.

XO Cardigan

XO patterns are found in textile design from Ireland to Africa. Many ancient civilizations used the X and O to represent the sun and moon, male and female, the attraction of opposites. Even the simple game of tic-tac-toe uses the X and O as opposing symbols. The joining of opposites creates balance, and in the world of design the combination of X and O creates a pleasing and balanced visual effect.

Finished Sizes	Chest	Length
Size A	40" (101.5 cm)	22½" (57 cm)
Size B	44" (112 cm)	24" (61 cm)
Size C	48" (122 cm)	25½" (65 cm)
Size D	52" (132 cm)	27½" (70 cm)

Yarn: Blackwater Abbey (100% wool; 220 yds [201 m]/3.5 oz [100 g]): Silver, 5 skeins

Needles: 24" (60-cm) circular size 5 (3.75 mm) for A, size 6 (4 mm) for B, size 7 (4.5 mm) for C, size 8 (5 mm) for D. 16" (40-cm) circular one size smaller than needle used for body. Adjust needle size if necessary to obtain the correct gauge.

Notions: Eight ⅝" (16 mm) buttons; stitch markers; stitch holders; cable needle

Gauge in Stockinette stitch on larger needle
    Size A: 20 sts and 32 rows = 4" (10 cm)
    Size B: 18 sts and 30 rows = 4" (10 cm)
    Size C: 17 sts and 28 rows = 4" (10 cm)
    Size D: 16 sts and 26 rows = 4" (10 cm)
    Remember: Gauge determines how your garment will fit. Swatch until you get it right.

SEED STITCH
Worked back and forth over an odd number of sts: *K1, p1; repeat from *, to last st, k1.
Worked circularly over an odd number of sts:
Round 1: *K1, p1; repeat from *, end k1.
Round 2: *P1, k1; repeat from *, end p1.

BACK AND FRONTS
Back and fronts are worked in one piece to underarm.

Work first 7 and last 7 sts of each row in seed st for front bands. Buttonholes are made in right front as vest is knit.

    Cast on 231 sts. Work k1, p1 for 1 row.
Next Row: Work in seed st, increasing 14 sts as follows: seed st 12, inc 1, *seed st 16, inc 1, repeat from * to last 11 sts, seed st to end—245 sts on needle.
Next Row (RS): Work row 1 of chart. Place buttonholes on pattern row 3 (RS row) and every 24 rows thereafter—6 buttonholes total.

    Make buttonholes as follows: At beginning of row, pattern 3 sts, k2 tog, yo, pattern 2 sts.

    Work through row 16 of chart. Work rows 1–16 of chart 5 more times.

DIVIDE FOR UNDERARMS
Next Row (row 1 of chart): Work in pattern as established, placing markers between 63rd and 64th sts and between 182nd and 183rd sts to mark underarms.
Next Row (row 2 of chart): Work in pattern to 10 sts past first marker and place last 20 sts worked (including marker) on holder for left underarm. Work to 10 sts past second marker and place last 20 sts worked (including marker) on holder for right underarm. Work to end of row. Do not break yarn. Place both fronts on holders, leaving only center 99 sts on needle for back.

BACK
Attach new yarn. Keeping pattern as established, complete rows 4–16 of chart, work rows 1–16 four more times, and then work rows 1–6 once more. Place sts on holder.

LEFT FRONT
Place left-front sts on needle. Attach new yarn. Keeping pattern as established, complete rows 4–16 of chart, work rows 1–16 two more times, then work rows 1–15 once more.

Shape Neck

Next Row (row 16 of chart): Work to last 17 sts and put them on holder. Turn and work back.

Decrease Row (RS): Work in pattern to last 3 sts, k2tog, k1. Work this decrease row every other row 3 more times—32 sts left on needle.

Continue in pattern as established until front has same number of rows as back, ending with row 6. Place sts on holder.

RIGHT FRONT

Note: Remember to keep 7 front edge sts in seed st and continue making buttonholes until there are 6 buttonholes total.

Place right-front sts with yarn attached on needle. Keeping pattern as established, complete rows 4–16 of chart, work rows 1–16 two more times, then work rows 1–15 once more. After last row, break yarn.

Shape Neck

Next Row (row 16 of chart): Place first 17 sts on holder. Attach yarn and work remaining sts in pattern as established. Turn and work back.

Decrease Row (RS): K1, ssk, work in pattern to end of row. Work this decrease row every other row 3 more times—32 sts left on needle.

Continue in pattern as established until front has same number of rows as back, ending with row 6. Place sts on holder.

SHOULDERS

Bind off shoulders together (see three-needle bind-off on page 127), making sure that patterns match.

NECKBAND

Note: Be sure to keep first 7 sts of right front and last 7 sts of left front in seed st when picking up to avoid a visible break in pattern. With smaller 16" (40-cm) needle, attach yarn and work 17 sts from right-front holder.

Pick up by knitting 17 sts up right-front neck to shoulder, knit 35 back neck sts, pick up by knitting 17 sts down left-front neck, work 17 sts from left-front holder—103 sts on needle. Turn and work in seed st for 10 rows. Bind off loosely in pattern.

ARMBANDS

With smaller 16" (40-cm) needle and starting at middle of underarm, pick by knitting 103 sts around armhole. Join and work circularly in seed st for 3 rounds. Bind off loosely in pattern.

FINISHING

Weave in all ends. Wash and block.

Buttons

Sew buttons opposite buttonholes on left front.

Lapels

Fold top corners of front bands down at a right angle to front edge and tack down with buttons.

☐ **knit on RS; purl on WS**

⊡ **purl on RS; knit on WS**

⧄ **2/2 Right Cross: place 2 sts on cn to back, k2, k2 from cn**

⧄ **2/2 Left Cross: place 2 sts on cn to front, k2, k2 from cn**

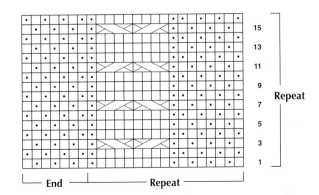

Celtic Lattice

Inspired by designs in historic manuscripts, Celtic Lattice has the advantage of looking very complicated while being quite pleasant and rhythmical to knit.

Finished Sizes
(buttoned, including borders)

	Chest	Length
Size A	40¼" (102 cm)	19¾" (50 cm)
Size B	43¾" (111 cm)	21¼" (54 cm)
Size C	48" (122 cm)	23" (58.5 cm)

Yarn: Cheryl Oberle's Dancing Colors™ Hand-dyed yarn (50% merino/50% mohair, 490 yd [448 m]/ 8 oz hank): Azurine, 1 hank; sportweight wool (550 yd [503 m]): Black

Needles: 24" (60-cm) circular size 3 (3.25 mm) for A, size 4 (3.5 mm) for B, size 5 (3.75 mm) for C. 24" (60-cm) and 16" (40-cm) circular needles two sizes smaller than needle used for body. Adjust needle size if necessary to obtain the correct gauge.

Notions: Seven ½" (12 mm) buttons; stitch markers; stitch holders

Gauge in two-color pattern on larger needle (see page 128 for two-color swatching instructions).
Size A: 24 stitches and 28 rows = 4" (10 cm)
Size B: 22 stitches and 26 rows = 4" (10 cm)
Size C: 20 stitches and 24 rows = 4" (10 cm)
Remember: Gauge determines how your garment will fit. Swatch until you get it right.

Except for bottom border facing, vest is worked circularly up to shoulders. Steeks are made for center front, armholes, and neck opening (see page 129 for an explanation of steeks). Work in stockinette stitch using the two-color stranding technique (see page 128).

Bottom Border and Facing

The border is worked in St st with a facing. The facing is worked flat and, once completed, sts are joined with a steek to begin circular knitting.

With smaller 24" (60-cm) needle and black, use provisional cast-on (see page 124) to cast on 234 sts.

Work 12 rows of St st (knit one row, purl one row) ending with a purl row.

Folding Ridge
Change to larger 24" (60-cm) needle and purl next (RS) row. *Do not turn.*

Steek and Join
Place marker for beginning of steek. Make a steek by

casting 3 sts onto right needle (needle with yarn attached) using the backward loop method (see page 124). Place marker for end of steek. When knitting steeks, alternate the colors on every st and every round.

Being careful not to twist sts, join into round by knitting into first st on left needle. This st is the first st of each round.

Place markers for underarms between 58th and 59th st and between 176th and 177th stitch.

MAIN COLOR PATTERN

There are 58 sts for each front and 118 sts for the back (counted between steek and underarm markers for fronts and between underarm markers for back).

Work charts A and B as follows: Work A, B, A, B, A to center back, then work A, B, A, B, A to end of round. Keeping chart B as established, work rounds 1–30 of chart A once, then rounds 13–30 (the 18-round repeat marked on the chart) twice.

RESERVE UNDERARM STITCHES

Next Round: Work to 13 sts before first underarm marker. Place next 27 sts, including marker, on holder.

MAKE ARMHOLE STEEKS

Place marker for beginning of steek. Cast on 3 sts on right needle using the backward loop method. Place marker for end of steek. Join again by knitting into next st on left needle.

Knit to 14 sts before second underarm marker. Place next 27 sts, including marker, on holder.

Make second armhole steek just like the first, placing markers on each side of steek sts.

Knit to end of round—189 stitches on needle including steeks.

SHAPE ARMHOLES

Decreases for armhole shaping are worked on either side of each armhole steek. Remember to alternate the colors on steek sts.

ARMHOLE DECREASES

Next Round: Knit to 3 sts before first armhole steek, k2tog, k1, knit the steek sts, k1, ssk. Knit to 3 sts before second armhole steek, k2tog, k1, knit the steek sts, k1, ssk, knit to end of round. Work these decreases every other round 6 more times (7 times total)—161 sts on needle including steeks.

Work in established pattern through round 30 of chart A, then work rounds 13–30 once more. Break off yarns.

RESERVE NECK STITCHES AND MAKE NECK STEEK

Place center 35 sts (16 sts on each side of center steek and center steek sts) on holder.

Next Round (round 13 of chart A): At right front, reattach yarns and, maintaining pattern as established, complete round. At end of round, place a marker on right needle and cast on 3 sts for neck steek. Place another marker on right needle and join to resume circular knitting. Keeping pattern as established, work one more round.

SHAPE NECK

Next Round (round 15 of chart A): Decrease 1 st at each side of neck steek as follows: k1, ssk, knit to 3 sts before neck steek, k2tog, k1. Repeat this decrease every other round 2 more times (3 times total)—123 sts on needle including steeks.

Continue in pattern as established until 2 full repeats of rounds 13–30 of chart A have been completed above neckline. Place all sts on holder.

STITCHING AND CUTTING

Machine stitch and cut the steek for front opening, neck, and both armholes (see page 129).

SHOULDERS

Reserve 18 sts for each shoulder, front and back. Bind off the shoulders together (see three-needle bind-off on page 128). Keep center 42 sts on holder for back neck.

BUTTON AND BUTTONHOLE BANDS

With smaller 24" (60-cm) needle and black, begin above facing on right front and pick up by knitting 75 sts along right-front edge. Turn and purl 1 row (WS).

Begin chart C. **Note:** Since you are working back and forth (not circularly), read odd-numbered (RS) rows from right to left, and even-numbered (WS) rows from left to right.

Follow chart C, working buttonholes on rows 3 and 4 of chart as follows.

Buttonholes

Row 3: In pattern, k3, (yo) twice, k2tog, *k11, (yo) twice, k2tog; repeat from * 4 more times, knit to end of row.

Row 4: Purl in pattern, working double yarn overs as one stitch (drop the extra loop of double yarn over).

Rows 5–9: Complete chart C.

Folding Ridge

With black, knit the next (WS) row.

Border Facing

With black and starting with a knit row, work 4 more rows of St st, ending with a purl row.

Chart A

☐ Black

◇ Azurine

Chart B

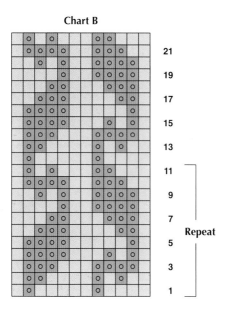

21

19

17

15

13

11

9

7   **Repeat**

5

3

1

Chart C

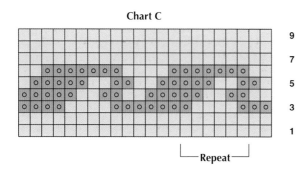

9

7

5

3

1

Repeat

Buttonholes in Facing

Row 7: Knit 3, (yo) twice, k2tog, *k11, (yo) twice, k2tog; repeat from * 4 more times, knit to end of row.

Row 8: Purl, working double yarn overs as one stitch (drop the extra loop of double yarnover). When facing buttonholes are complete, work 8 more rows of St st. Place sts on holder. Turn border facing to WS at folding ridge and tack down live sts to inside, covering cut edge of steek. Be sure to match up the buttonholes.

Buttonband

Pick up by knitting 75 sts along left-front edge and work as for buttonhole band but stay in pattern and do not make buttonholes on rows 3 and 4. When border facing is complete, place sts on holder. Turn border facing to WS at folding ridge and tack down live sts to inside, covering cut edge of steek.

NECKBAND

Using smaller 24" (60-cm) needle and black and beginning at top of right-front band, pick up by knitting 133 sts around neck edge as follows: pick up 6 sts across top edge of right-front band, 16 sts from right-front neck holder, 25 sts to shoulder, 39 sts from back-neck holder (decreasing 3 sts), 25 sts from shoulder to left-front neck holder, 16 sts from left-front neck holder, and 6 sts across top of left-front band. Turn and purl one row. **Note:** Since you are working back and forth (not circularly), read odd-numbered (RS) rows from right to left, and even-numbered (WS) rows from left to right.

Buttonhole

Follow chart D, working a buttonhole on rows 9 and 10 of chart as follows.

Row 9: In pattern, k3, (yo) twice, k2tog, knit in pattern to end of row.

Row 10: Purl in pattern, working double yarnover as one stitch (drop the extra loop of double yarn over).

Complete chart D.

Folding Ridge

With black, knit the next (WS) row.

Border Facing

With black and starting with a knit row, work 4 rows of St st, ending with a purl row.

Buttonhole in Facing

Row 1: Knit 3, (yo) twice, k2tog, knit in pattern to end of row.

Row 2: Purl, working double yarn over as one stitch (drop the extra loop of double yarn over).

When facing buttonhole is complete, work 13 more rows of St st. Place sts on holder. Turn border facing to WS at purl row and tack down live sts to inside, covering cut edge of steek. Be sure to match up buttonholes.

ARMHOLE BANDS

Armhole bands are worked circularly in St st with a facing.

With smaller 16" (40-cm) needle and black, begin at middle of underarm and pick up by knitting 121 sts around armhole including underarm sts. Join and knit 1 round. Work rows 1–9 of chart C.

Folding Ridge

With black, purl the next round.

Facing

With black, knit 12 rounds. Turn facing to WS at folding ridge and tack down live sts to inside, covering cut edge of steek.

FINISHING

Remove provisional cast-on and tack down live sts to inside. Weave in all ends. Wash and block. Sew on buttons opposite buttonholes.

Chart D

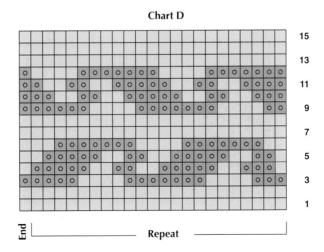

ʃtone Walls

The rich fields of Ireland are fenced with low walls made of the stones gathered while clearing the land. These walls create beautiful patchwork patterns in the landscape. It is said that in Irish knitting, the diamond lattice represents both prosperity and the stone walls surrounding the fields of western Ireland.

Finished Sizes	Chest	Length
Size A	38" (96.5 cm)	24½" (62 cm)
Size B	44½" (113 cm)	26½" (67.5 cm)
Size C	51" (129.5 cm)	27½" (70 cm)

Yarn: Black Water Abbey (100% wool; 220 yd [201 m]/3.5 oz [100 g]): Bracken, 4 (4, 5) skeins.

Needles: 24" (60-cm) circular size 8 (5 mm); 24" (60-cm) and 16" (40-cm) circular needles two sizes smaller than needle used for body. Adjust needle size if necessary to obtain the correct gauge.

Notions: Markers; stitch holders; cable needle

Gauge in Stockinette stitch on larger needle
   17 sts and 25 rows = 4" (10 cm)
   Remember: Gauge determines how your garment will fit. Swatch until you get it right.

Note: The slipover is worked circularly to the underarms and then divided and the back and fronts are worked separately.

The Aran stitch patterns pull in until the garment is blocked. When blocking, follow the hand-washing instructions on page 125 and gently stretch the wet fabric open to obtain measurements of desired size. Pin in place to hold. The measurements taken while knitting take this expansion into account. Just be sure to get the correct gauge in stockinette stitch and everything should work out fine.

BOTTOM BORDER

With smaller 24" (60-cm) needle, cast on 164 (184, 204) sts.

Being sure that your sts are not twisted, place marker and join by knitting into first st on left needle. This st is the first st of each round and the center of left underarm. Work 82 (92, 102) sts in k2, p2 ribbing and place marker for right underarm. Continue in ribbing to end of round. Work ribbing for 2½" (6 cm).

Change to larger needle and set up pattern as follows:

Round 1: *Work 21 (26, 31) sts of chart, pm, m1 (count this m1 increase as the first st of cable section of chart); work cable section of chart to last st, m1 (count this m1 increase as the last st of cable section of chart), pm; work 21 (26, 31) sts of chart, repeat from * to end of round—168 (188, 208) sts on the needle.

Continue in pattern as established until body measures 11½ (12½, 13½)" (29 [32, 34] cm) (short version: 6 (7½, 8½)" [15 (19, 21.5) cm]) above ribbing, ending with an even-numbered round.

RESERVE UNDERARM STITCHES

Next Round: Work to 5 (9, 13) sts after right underarm marker. Place last 10 (18, 26) sts on holder for right underarm; work the next 74 (76, 78) sts for back; work to 5 (9, 13) sts after left underarm marker. Place last 10 (18, 26) sts on holder for left underarm and remaining 74 (76, 78) sts on holder for front. Turn and work pattern as established for 1 row.

Note: The knitting is now back and forth, not circular; read even-numbered rows of charts from left to right and odd-numbered rows from right to left.

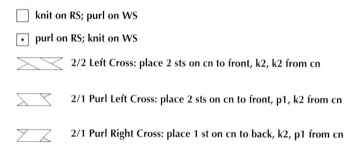

☐ knit on RS; purl on WS

⊡ purl on RS; knit on WS

2/2 Left Cross: place 2 sts on cn to front, k2, k2 from cn

2/1 Purl Left Cross: place 2 sts on cn to front, p1, k2 from cn

2/1 Purl Right Cross: place 1 st on cn to back, k2, p1 from cn

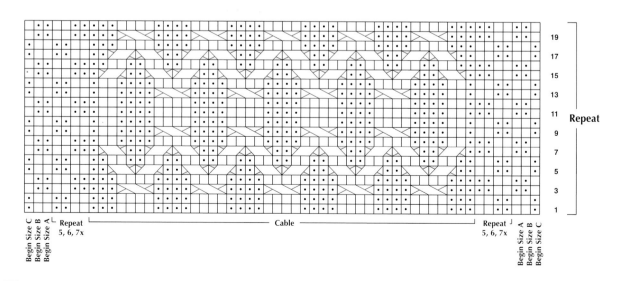

BACK

Shape Armhole

Next Row (RS): K1, ssk, work to last 3 sts, k2tog, k1. Repeat these decreases every other row 5 more times—62 (64, 66) sts left on needle. Work in established pattern until back measures 10½ (11½, 11½)" (26.5 [29, 29] cm) from underarm. Place all sts on holder.

FRONT

Work as for back until armhole shaping is complete and front measures 7½ (8, 8)" (19 [20, 20] cm) from underarm, ending with an even-numbered row.

Neck Shaping

Next Row (RS): Work in pattern over 15 (15, 16) sts. Place the next 32 (34, 34) sts on holder for neck and the following 15 (15, 16) sts on holder for right front.

LEFT FRONT

Turn and work back in pattern.

Next Row (RS): Work to last 3 sts, k2tog, k1. Repeat this decrease row every other row 3 more times. Work even until armhole measures 10½ (11½, 11½)" (26.5 [29, 29] cm) from underarm. Place sts on holder.

RIGHT FRONT

Place sts on needle. Beginning with a RS row, work 2 rows in pattern.

Next Row (RS): K1, ssk, work in pattern to end. Repeat this decrease row every other row 3 more times. Work even until armhole measures 10½ (11½, 11½)" (26.5 [29, 29] cm) from underarm. Place sts on holder.

SHOULDERS

Reserve 12 (12, 13) sts for each shoulder, front and back. Bind off shoulders together (see three-needle bind-off on page 127). Keep center 38 (40, 40) sts on holder for back neck.

NECKBAND

With smaller 16" (40-cm) needle and beginning at left shoulder, pick up by knitting 9 (13, 13) sts down to front neck, knit the 32 (34, 34) front neck sts, pick up by knitting 9 (13, 13) sts up right front, knit the 38 (40, 40) back neck sts. 88 (100, 100) sts on needle. Join and work in k2, p2 ribbing for 5 rows. Bind off in ribbing.

ARMHOLE BANDS

With smaller 16" (40-cm) needle and beginning at the middle of the underarm, pick up by knitting 88 (100, 104) sts around armhole including the underarm sts on holder. Join and work in k2, p2 ribbing for 6 rounds. Bind off in ribbing.

FINISHING

Weave in all ends. Wash and block.

6

Peru

In Peru, knitting is an activity pursued by all ages of both sexes. In fact, many of the beautiful Ch'ullu hats that are an icon of Peruvian knitting are knitted by men for themselves and their children. As part of their traditional clothing, Peruvians also knit wonderfully patterned and brightly colored forearm coverings, leggings, and small bags.

Bayeta

A popular style of vest worn in Peru is made from a handwoven wool cloth called *bayeta*, from a Spanish word meaning felt or flannel. Great embellishers, Peruvians often trim these simple vests with patterned bands. The pattern on the band of Bayeta is from a knitted Ch'ullu in my personal collection.

Finished Sizes

Finished Sizes	Chest	Length
Size A	38½" (98 cm)	19" (48.5 cm)
Size B	42" (106.5 cm)	21" (53.5 cm)
Size C	46½" (118 cm)	23" (58.5 cm)

Yarn: Rocky Mountain Llama Fiber Pool (100% alpaca, 2 oz [57 g] hanks): Black (Color A) 8 hanks (approximately 175 yd [160 m] each); Dark Fawn (Color B) 1 hank (approximately 155 yd [142 m]); Dark Red Brown (Color C) 2 hanks (approximately 140 yd [128 m] each). Rocky Mountain Llama Fiber Pool (80% alpaca/20% tussah silk 175 yd [160 m]/2 oz [57 g]): Off-white (Color D) 1 hank. **Note:** Only a small amount of this color is needed, about 30 yd (27 m); you may substitute a small amount of any off-white fingering or sportweight yarn. If using

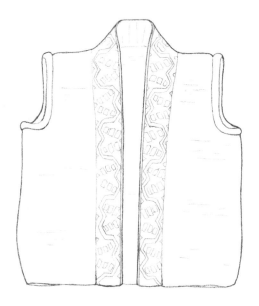

sportweight yarn as a substitute, use a single strand.

Needles: 24" (60-cm) circular size 3 (3.25 mm) for A, size 4 (3.5 mm) for B, size 5 (3.75 mm) for C. 24" (60-cm) and 16" (40-cm) circular needles one size smaller than needle used for body. Adjust needle size if necessary to obtain the correct gauge.

Notions: Stitch markers; stitch holders

Gauge in Garter stitch on larger needle
   Size A: 22 sts and 44 rows = 4" (10 cm)
   Size B: 20 sts and 40 rows = 4" (10 cm)
   Size C: 18 sts and 36 rows = 4" (10 cm)

Bayeta is sized by gauge; be sure to get the correct stitch gauge for the chosen size. Measure knitting while piece is lying flat on a solid surface. Do not stretch to measure. The weight of the alpaca will make the garment drop in length when hanging and give an inaccurate measurement. The stranded two-color front band stabilizes the shape of the vest.

Yarns are used double throughout except where otherwise specified. Wind two hanks at a time and hold strands from both balls together while knitting. For a single hank, wind two approximately equal balls and use a strand from both balls, being careful not to drop one of the strands as you are knitting. **Note:** When counting rows in garter stitch, one ridge equals two rows.

BACK AND FRONTS
Back and fronts are worked in one piece to underarm. With 2 strands color A and larger needle, cast on 183 sts.
Note: Place marker on right side to indicate right from wrong side.
Row 1 (RS): Knit, placing underarm markers between the 39th and 40th sts and between the 144th and 145th sts.
   Work in garter st for 132 rows, ending with a RS row.

DIVIDE FOR UNDERARMS
Next Row (WS): Knit to 7 sts past first marker, place last 14 sts worked (including marker) on holder for left underarm. Knit to 7 sts past second marker and place last 14 sts worked (including marker) on holder for right underarm. Work to end of row. Place both fronts on holders, leaving only center 91 sts on needle for back.

BACK
Shape Armholes
Next Row (RS): Attach new yarn and knit, decreasing 1 st at each armhole edge as follows: K1, ssk, knit to last 3 sts, k2tog, k1. Repeat this shaping every other row 6 more times (7 times total)—

77 sts on needle. Work in garter st for 106 rows, ending with a WS row. Place back sts on holder.

LEFT FRONT

Place left-front sts on needle. Attach yarn. Shape armhole and neck as follows.

Next Row (RS): K1, ssk (armhole decrease), knit to last 3 sts, k2tog, k1 (neck decrease). Repeat armhole shaping every other row 6 more times; repeat neck shaping every 12th row 8 more times—16 sts on needle. Work in garter st for 106 rows, ending with a RS row. Place sts on holder.

RIGHT FRONT

Place right-front sts on needle. Attach yarn. Shape armhole and neck as follows.

Next Row (RS): K1, ssk (neck decrease), knit to last 3 sts, k2tog, k1 (armhole decrease). Repeat armhole shaping every other row 6 more times; repeat neck shaping every 12th row 8 more times—16 sts on the needle. Work in garter st for 106 rows, ending with a RS row. Place sts on holder.

SHOULDERS

With right sides held together, bind off shoulder seams together (see page 127 for three-needle bind-off).

■ Black (Color A)

☐ Dark Fawn (Color B)

▨ Dark Red Brown (Color C)

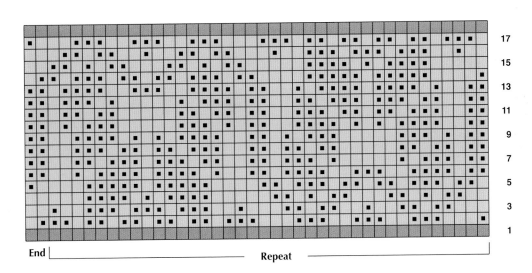

End | Repeat

FRONT/NECK BORDERS

Borders are worked in St st with a facing. They may be worked flat (back and forth) or circularly.

Worked Flat

With color A, smaller 24" (60-cm) needle, and beginning at bottom of right front, pick up by knitting 112 sts to shoulder, knit 45 sts from back neck holder decreasing one st, and pick up by knitting 112 to bottom of left front—268 sts on needle. Turn.

Next Row: (WS) *K2 with color C, k2 with color D; repeat from *. Break off color D. Turn and work 18 rows of chart.

Folding Ridge

When chart is complete, purl the next (RS) row with two strands of color C.

Border Facing

With *one strand only* of color C and beginning with a purl row, work 20 rows of St st. Tack down live sts of facing to inside.

Worked Circularly

See page 129 for steek techniques. At the end of row 1 of chart do not turn, place marker on needle, cast on 8 sts for steek, place another marker on needle, join to beginning of round making sure band sts are not twisted on needle. Work circularly (read all rounds from right to left) for the rest of the chart. Remember to alternate the colors in the steek on every st and every round.

Folding Ridge

When chart is completed, purl one round with 2 strands of color C. Cut through the steek sts. Machine stitch if necessary (see page 129).

Border Facing

With *one strand only* of color C, work 20 rows of St st. Place all sts on holder. Fold extra sts up into inside of border and tack end of border closed.

Tack down live sts of facing to inside.

ARMHOLE BANDS

These are knitted circularly in St st and roll to right side of vest.

With 16" (40-cm) circular needle and *one strand only* of color C, pick up by knitting 109 sts around the armhole as follows: beginning at middle of underarm, place first 7 sts on the needle and knit them, pick up by knitting 47 sts to shoulder, pick up by knitting 1 st from shoulder, pick up by knitting 47 sts to the last 7 sts on underarm holder, place these sts on needle and knit. Join and knit 11 rounds. Bind off loosely and allow band to roll toward body.

FINISHING

Weave in all ends. Wash and block.

7

Japan

Wabi-Sabi is a Japanese term for a way of life that focuses on the simple, everyday, overlooked details of life and nature. Beauty is not only found in the new and perfect but also in the worn and used items of daily life. Associated with the Japanese tea ceremony, Wabi-Sabi is more than just an academic theory of beauty; it is a spiritual and material path to being present in the beauty of the moment.

Sakiori

The country folk of Japan are masters of recycling. Clothing and cloth are used and reused, patched and transformed until there is nothing left, so nothing is wasted. Even beautiful kimonos, traditionally associated with the aristocratic classes in Japan, find their way into the lives of the country people. Pieces of worn-out garments made from wonderful cloth are used to make work clothes in a method known as *sakiori*. Sakiori means tear and weave or torn weaving and consists of narrow pieces of fabric woven from worn garments torn into thin strips and used as weft. The resulting randomly striped fabric makes warm and sturdy vests. Many pieces of sakiori use the blues of the indigo-dyed cloth commonly worn in the country. Other sakiori weavings use more colorful pieces of cotton or silk. Each piece of sakiori cloth is unique and the artistry of the weaver shows in the choosing of the color combinations.

The horizontal patterning of sakiori cloth lends itself nicely to knitting and the practice of random coloring can help the knitter develop her own sense of color. The Sakiori Vests are simple stockinette-stitch vests using random stripes. As is traditional, the vests are made from two strips of cloth seamed at the back and connected with side panels. It is a belief that the seam in the back acts as a charm to protect the wearer.

ʃakiori I (Long version)

This is a simple stockinette stitch vest with random stripes and side extension panels. Colors of yarns are randomly changed to form multi-colored stripes.

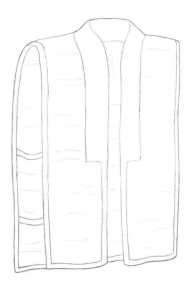

Finished Sizes	Chest	Length
Size A	42" (106.5 cm)	29" (73.5 cm)
Size B	44" (112 cm)	31" (78.5 cm)
Size C	48" (122 cm)	32" (81.5 cm)

Yarn: Rowan Felted Tweed (50% merino/25% alpaca/ 25% viscose, 190 yd [175 m]/1¾ oz [50g]): color #131 (A), 7 skeins; #141 (B), 7 skeins; colors #134 (C) and #139 (D), 1 skein each.

Needles: Straight or 24" (60-cm) circular size 8 (5 mm). 29" (72-cm) circular needle two sizes smaller than needle used for body. Adjust needle size if necessary to obtain the correct gauge.

Notions: Stitch holders

Gauge in Stockinette stitch on larger needle
    16 sts and 24 rows = 4" (10 cm)

SEED STITCH
Row 1: *K1, p1; repeat from *.
Row 2: *P1, k1; repeat from *.
    Repeat Rows 1 and 2 for pattern.

BACK
The back is worked in two narrow panels that are later sewn together.

Left Back Panel
With smaller needle and two strands of color A, cast on 36 sts. Work in seed st for 10 rows. Change to larger needle and work in St st in the following color sequence: (This is a possible color sequence but feel free to work your own. It's supposed to be random.) Yarns are used double throughout.

Row 1: AA	*Rows 50–58:* AB
Rows 2–6: AB	*Rows 59–61:* BC
Rows 7–11: AA	*Rows 62–63:* AA
Rows 12–14: BB	*Rows 64–65:* BC
Rows 15–18: BC	*Rows 66–67:* AB
Rows 19–20: BD	*Rows 68–72:* BB
Rows 21–26: AC	*Rows 73–78:* AB
Rows 27–30: AB	*Rows 79–80:* BB
Rows 31–39: BB	*Rows 81–83:* AC
Rows 40–41: AB	*Rows 84–88:* BD
Rows 42–45: BB	*Rows 89–93:* AB
Row 46: AB	*Rows 94–97:* BB
Rows 47–49: BB	*Rows 98–101:* BB

Continue to combine the colors using A and B mostly and C and D in combination with A and B on occasion.

Work until Left Back Panel measures 29 (31, 32)" (73.5 [78.5, 81.5] cm). Place sts on holder.

Right Back
Work as for Left Back but change the striping pattern. The stripes are not supposed to match or be symmetrical down the center back.

FRONTS (make 2)
Keeping the striping random, work as for Backs until pieces measure 14" (35.5 cm), ending on a right-side row.

Left Front
Bind off 14 sts and work to end of row. Continue on the remaining 22 sts until piece measures 29 (31, 32)" (73.5 [78.5, 81.5] cm) from the cast-on edge. Place sts on holder.

Right Front
Work one WS row. *Next Row (RS):* Bind off 14 sts and work to end of row. Continue on the remaining 22 sts until piece measures 29 (31, 32)" (73.5 [78.5, 81.5] cm) from cast-on edge. Place sts on holder.

SIDE PANELS (make 2)
With smaller needle and two strands of color A, cast on 16 (20, 28) sts. Work seed st for 6 rows. Change to larger needle and work in random stripe pattern until piece measures 9" (23 cm) from beginning. Change to smaller needle and work seed st for 6 rows. Bind off loosely in pattern.

Sew back panels together. Bind off the shoulders together (see three-needle bind-off on page 127).

SIDE BORDERS
With smaller needle, RS facing, and beginning at lower right back, use two strands of color A to pick up by knitting 232 (248, 256) sts up the back and down to the lower right front (pick up in two rows and skip a row). Work in seed st for 6 rows. Bind off loosely in pattern. Repeat on other side edge beginning at lower left front.

ATTACH SIDE PANELS
With top of side panels 13 (14, 15)" (33 [35.5, 38] cm) down from shoulder seam, join panels to vest by sewing the edges along the line where you picked up stitches—the side borders overlap the panels.

NECK BORDER
Neck border is worked in seed st in one piece from the right-front bound-off sts to shoulder seam, along back neck and down to left-front bound-off sts.

With RS facing, pick up by knitting 60 (68, 72) sts along right front (pick up in two rows and skip a row), 26 sts across the back neck, and 60 (68, 72) sts along left front—146 (162, 170) sts.

Work 20 rows in seed st, place sts on holder. Sew neck border to bound-off sts.

With 29" (72-cm) needle, RS facing, and beginning at lower right front, pick up by knitting 56 sts from bottom of right front to neck border sts on hold. Knit the 146 (162, 170) sts of neck border, pick up by knitting 56 sts along left front to bottom edge—258 (274, 282) sts total. Work in seed st for 6 more rows. Bind off loosely in pattern.

FINISHING
Weave in all ends. Wash and block.

∫akiori II (Short version)

This is a simple stockinette-stitch vest with random stripes and side extension panels. The yarn used is randomly dyed and colors are randomly changed to form the multicolored stripes.

Finished Sizes	Chest	Length
Size A	42" (106.5 cm)	20" (51 cm)
Size B	44" (112 cm)	22" (56 cm)
Size C	48" (122 cm)	23" (58.5 cm)

Yarn: La Lana Wools Forever Random© Blends (wool and mohair blends, 80 yd/2 oz): Color A (Apassionada), 3 skeins; Color B (Potpourri), 3 skeins; Color C (Te Morada), 2 skeins; Color D (Safari Day), 1 skein; Color E (Florence's Blend), 1 skein; Color F (Deep Sea Indigo), 2 skeins

Needles: 24" (60-cm) circular size 8 (5 mm). 29" (72-cm) circular needle two sizes smaller than needle used for body. Adjust needle size if necessary to obtain the correct gauge.

Notions: Stitch holders

Gauge in stockinette stitch on larger needle
    14 sts and 22 rows = 4" (10 cm)

Colors are changed randomly throughout the garment. Work one to six rows of a color before changing. Random too hard? Try this. Assign numbers to each color from one to six. Using two dice, assign one to be the color chooser and the other to be the row number chooser. Roll the color chooser to pick a color and then roll the row chooser to determine how many rows to do of the chosen color.

Change color in seed stitch just as for stockinette stitch sections.

SEED STITCH
Row 1: *K1, p1; repeat from *.
Row 2: *P1, k1; repeat from *.
    Repeat rows 1 and 2 for pattern.

BACK
The back is worked in two narrow panels that are later sewn together.

Left Back Panel
With smaller needle and color A, cast on 30 sts. Work in seed st for 10 rows. Change to larger needle and work random stripes in St st. Work until Left Back Panel measures 20 (22, 23)" (51 [56, 58.5] cm. Place sts on holder.

Right Back Panel
Work as for Left Back but change the striping pattern. The stripes are not supposed to match or be symmetrical down the center back.

FRONTS (make 2)

Keeping the striping random, work as for Backs until pieces measure 5½" (14 cm) ending on a RS row.

Left Front

Work 12 sts and place them on holder. Work to end of row. Continue on remaining 18 sts until piece measures 20 (22, 23)" (51 [56, 58.5] cm) from cast-on edge. Place sts on holder.

Right Front

Work next row and place last 12 sts on holder. Continue on remaining 18 sts until piece measures 20 (22, 23)" (51 [56, 58.5] cm) from cast-on edge. Place sts on holder.

SIDE PANELS (make 2)

With smaller needle and color A, cast on 18 (22, 28) sts. Work in random-colored seed st for 9 rows. Change to larger needle and work St st in random stripe pattern for 5½" (14 cm). Change to smaller needle and work random-colored seed st for 9 rows. Bind off loosely in pattern.

Sew back panels together. Bind off shoulders together (see three-needle bind-off on page 127).

SIDE BORDERS

With smaller needle, color A, RS facing, and beginning at lower right back, pick up by knitting 160 (176, 184) sts up the back and down to lower right front (pick up in two rows and skip a row). Work in random-colored seed st for 7 rows. Bind off loosely in pattern. Repeat on other side edge beginning at lower left front.

ATTACH SIDE PANELS

With top of side panels 10½ (11½, 12½)" (26.5 [29, 32] cm) down from shoulder seam, join panels to vest by sewing the edges along the line where you picked up stitches—the side borders overlap the panels.

NECK BORDER

The neck border is worked in one piece from the right front sts on hold to shoulder seam, along back neck, and down to left front sts on hold.

With RS facing, pick up by knitting 51 (58, 61) sts along right front (pick up in two rows and skip a row), 22 sts across back neck, and 51 (58, 61) sts along left front—124 (138, 144) sts. Work in random-colored seed st for 24 rows, attaching neck border to front stitches on hold as follows beginning with a WS row:

Row 1: Seed st to last st, ssk last st with a st from holder, turn.

Row 2: Slip 1 as if to purl, seed st to last st, ssk it tog with a st from front holder, turn.

Repeat row 2 until all sts are used up from holders (24 rows). Place sts on holder.

With 29" (72-cm) needle, RS facing, and beginning at lower right front, pick up by knitting 20 sts from bottom of right front to neck border sts on hold, work neck border sts in seed st, pick up by knitting 20 sts along left front to bottom edge—164 (178, 184) sts total, turn. Bind off loosely.

FINISHING

Ties

Make two 5" (12.5 cm) braids or twisted cords and attach to inside at bottom of neck border.

Weave in all ends. Wash and block.

Kasuri Chanchanko

Kasuri is the Japanese form of ikat weaving. The yarns are resist dyed with indigo to create a pattern on the cloth after weaving. The traditional technique requires that the weft yarns be tightly wrapped with hemp bark before dyeing to create a specific pattern. Once woven, the resulting patterns have characteristic fuzzy or blurred edges. Kasuri has its roots in the garments of farmers whose skillful wives wove the fabrics on simple looms during the winter months. Kasuri garments were also very popular among the samurai and fashion conscious Japanese upper classes in the nineteenth and early twentieth centuries. Today only a few weavers have the skill to create the hand-dyed and handwoven kasuri cloth. These master weavers are considered to be national treasures in Japan and the kasuri fabric that they produce has become very collectible.

Finished Sizes	Chest	Length
Size A	41½" (105.5 cm)	22½" (57 cm)
Size B	44½" (113 cm)	24" (61 cm)
Size C	51½" (131 cm)	25½" (65 cm)

Yarn: Jamieson's 2-ply Shetland (100% Shetland wool [150 yd (137 m)/25 g]): Color A (#726 Prussian Blue), 5 skeins; Color B (#122 Granite), 3 skeins

Needles: 24" (60-cm) circular size 3 (3.25 mm) for A, size 4 (3.5 mm) for B, size 5 (3.75 mm) for C. 24" (60-cm) and 16" (40-cm) circular needles one size smaller than needle used for body. Adjust needle size if necessary to obtain the correct gauge.

Notions: Stitch markers; stitch holders

Gauge in two-color pattern on larger needle (see page 128 for two-color swatching instructions).
Size A: 28 sts and 34 rows = 4" (10 cm)
Size B: 26 sts and 32 rows = 4" (10 cm)
Size C: 24 sts and 30 rows = 4" (10 cm)

Notes: Adjust the number of stitches to accommodate the differing stitch multiples between patterns as indicated.

On the long carries of Pattern 2 catch the carried yarn (see page 128) at a different stitch on each row. The catches will show a bit but that will enhance the traditional tweedy look of kasuri fabric.

Except for the bottom border facing, the vest is worked circularly up to the shoulders. Steeks are made for the front opening and armholes (see page 129 for an explanation of steeks). Work in stockinette

stitch using the two-color stranding technique (see page 128).

BOTTOM BORDER AND FACING

The border is worked in St st with a facing. The facing is worked flat and after the facing is complete the sts will be joined to begin circular knitting.

With smaller 24" (60-cm) needle and color A, cast on 252 sts using a provisional cast-on (see page 124).

Work 10 rows of St st (knit one row, purl one row) ending with a purl row.

Folding Ridge
Change to larger 24" (60-cm) needle and purl the next (RS) row. *Do not turn.*

STEEK AND JOIN

Place marker for beginning of steek. Make a steek by casting 7 sts onto right needle (needle with yarn attached) using the backward loop method (see page 124). Place marker for end of steek. When knitting steeks, alternate colors on every st and every round.

Being careful not to twist sts, join into a round by knitting into first st on the left needle. This st is the first st of each round.

Knit first round, placing underarm markers between the 53rd and 54th sts and between the 199th and 200th sts—259 sts on needle.

MAIN COLOR PATTERN

Begin chart 1, working Pattern 1 two times. On first round of Pattern 2, decrease 1 st on each front and 3 sts evenly spaced across the back. *Note:* Work this decrease only for the first repeat of Pattern 2—254 sts on needle. Work Pattern 2 three times, then work 18 rounds of Pattern 2 once more. Remember to alternate colors in steek on every st and every round.

RESERVE UNDERARM STITCHES

Next Round (round 19 of Pattern 2): Work to 17 stitches before first underarm marker. Place next 34 sts, including marker, on holder.

MAKE ARMHOLE STEEKS

Place marker for beginning of steek. Cast on 7 sts on right needle using the backward loop method. Place marker for end of steek. Join again by knitting into next st on left needle.

Knit to 17 sts before second underarm marker. Place next 34 sts and underarm marker on holder.

Make second armhole steek just like the first, placing markers on each side of steek sts.

Knit to end of round—200 sts on needle including all steek sts.

SHAPE ARMHOLES

Decreases for armhole shaping are worked on either side of each armhole steek. Remember to alternate colors on the steek sts on two-color rounds.

Armhole Decreases
Next Round: (round 20 of Pattern 2) Knit to 3 sts before first armhole steek, k2tog, k1, knit steek sts, k1, ssk. Knit to 3 sts before second armhole steek, k2tog, k1, knit steek sts, k1, ssk, knit to end of round. Repeat these decreases every other round 2 more times (3 times total)—188 sts on needle including steeks. Work in established pattern until 5 full repeats of Pattern 2 have been completed, then work 10 rounds of Pattern 2 once more.

Begin chart 2. Work until chart 2 is complete. *Note:* After each steek, begin chart 2 at right edge.

STITCHING AND CUTTING

Machine stitch and cut the steek for the front opening, and both armholes (see page 129).

SHOULDERS

Reserve 32 sts for each shoulder, front and back. Bind

Chart 2

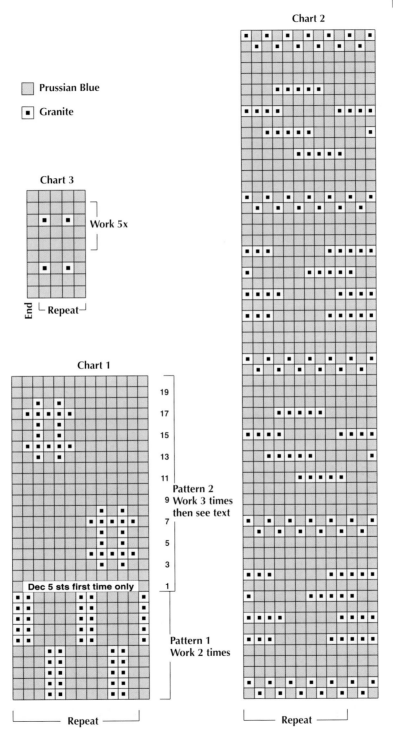

■ Prussian Blue

▪ Granite

Chart 3

Work 5x

End └ Repeat ┘

Chart 1

19
17
15
13
11

Pattern 2
9 Work 3 times
7 then see text
5
3
1

Dec 5 sts first time only

Pattern 1
Work 2 times

└───── Repeat ─────┘

└───── Repeat ─────┘

off shoulders together (see three-needle bind-off on page 127). Keep center 39 sts on holder for back neck.

FRONT/NECKBAND

With larger 24" (60-cm) needle and color A, begin at bottom of right front and pick up by knitting 135 sts along right-front edge. Knit the 39 back neck sts. Pick up by knitting 135 sts down left-front edge—309 sts on needle. Turn and purl one row. Begin chart 3 (RS). **Note:** Since you are working back and forth (not circularly), read the RS chart rows from right to left and the WS chart rows from left to right.

Complete chart 3.

Folding Ridge
With color A, knit the next (WS) row.

Border Facing
Change to smaller 24" (60-cm) needle and color A and, starting with a knit row, work 28 more rows of St st ending with a purl row. Turn border facing to WS at folding ridge and tack down live sts to inside, covering cut edge of steek.

ARMHOLE BANDS

Armhole bands are worked circularly in St st and roll toward RS of vest.

With smaller 16" (40-cm) needle and color A, begin at middle of underarm (last 17 sts on holder). *K2, k2tog; repeat from * 4 times; k1, pick up by knitting 46 sts up to shoulder and 46 sts down to underarm, work remaining 17 sts on holder as follows: k1, *k2, k2tog; repeat from * 4 times—118 sts on needle. Join and knit 12 rounds. Bind off loosely.

FINISHING

Bottom Hem
Remove provisional cast-on and tack down live sts to inside. Weave in ends. Wash and block.

8

Scandinavia

In Scandinavian folklore, light elves are the helpers of mankind. They bring good fortune and
health and they only ask that the hearth be swept and that fresh water be made available in which
they can bathe their children. It has also been said that elves love the gift of a few spare buttons,
but no metal buttons, please, as metal is disliked by almost all of the "good folk."

Scandinavian Star

The Scandinavian Star stitch pattern is a four-sided star in a diamond, a very traditional knitting pattern in Norway and Sweden. This design is also found in the knitting traditions of Estonia and Latvia and is believed by some to have originated in the patterns of Middle Eastern rugs.

Finished Sizes

Finished Sizes	Chest	Length
Size A	40" (101.5 cm)	19½" (49.5 cm)
Size B	44" (112 cm)	21" (53.5 cm)
Size C	48" (122 cm)	23" (58.5 cm)

Yarn: Rauma Strikkegarn (100% wool, 105 m [115 yd]/50 g [1.75 oz]): color #136 Black (Color A), 6 skeins; color #101 Off-white (Color B), 4 skeins.

Needles: 24" (60-cm) circular size 3 (3.25 mm) for A, size 4 (3.5 mm) for B, size 5 (3.75 mm) for C. 24" (60-cm) and 16" (40-cm) circular needles two sizes smaller than needle used for the body. Adjust needle size if necessary to obtain the correct gauge.

Notions: Four pewter clasp sets; stitch markers; stitch holders

Gauge in two-color pattern on larger needle (see page 128 for two-color swatching techniques).
Size A: 24 stitches and 28 rows = 4" (10 cm)
Size B: 22 stitches and 26 rows = 4" (10 cm)
Size C: 20 stitches and 24 rows = 4" (10 cm)

Except for the bottom border facing, the vest is worked circularly up to the shoulders. Steeks are made for the front opening and armholes. (See page 129 for working with steeks.) Work in stockinette stitch using the two-color stranding technique (see page 128), carrying the color not in use loosely across the back of the work. Do not carry the yarn over more than five stitches without catching it in the back.

BOTTOM BORDER AND FACING

The border is worked in St st with a facing. The facing is worked back and forth and once complete the sts are joined to begin circular knitting.

With smaller 24" (60-cm) needle and black, cast on provisionally (see page 124) 214 sts.

Work 12 rows of St st (knit one row, purl one row) ending with a purl row.

Folding Ridge
Change to larger 24" (60-cm) needle and purl the next (RS) row. Do not turn.

STEEK AND JOIN

Place marker and make steek by casting 5 sts with the backward loop method (see page 124) onto right needle (needle with yarn attached). Place marker on other side of steek. With black, knit one round.

BORDER PATTERN

Being sure that sts are not twisted, join by knitting into the first st on left needle. This is the first st of each round.

Knit round 1 of chart 1 and mark the sides by placing a marker between the 47th and 48th sts and between the 168th and 169th sts. Work through round 10. On round 11, increase 1 st after right side marker—220 sts on the needle including steek.

MAIN PATTERN

Follow chart 2, repeating rounds 1–24 twice, then work rounds 1–7 once more. Remember to alternate colors in steek on every st and every round.

RESERVE UNDERARM STITCHES

On round 8 of the third repeat, work to 12 sts before right side marker and place next 25 sts, including marker, on holder.

ARMHOLE STEEKS

Place marker and cast 5 sts onto right needle using the backward loop method. Place marker at end of steek. Join again by knitting into next st on left needle.

Knit to 13 sts before left-side marker and place next 25 sts, including marker, on holder.

Make second armhole steek just like the first, placing markers on each side of steek sts. Knit to end of round—180 sts on needle including steeks.

SHAPE ARMHOLES

Decreases for armhole shaping are worked on either side of each armhole steek. Remember to alternate colors on steek sts.

Knit to 3 sts before right armhole steek, k2tog, k1, knit steek sts, k1, ssk. Knit to 3 sts before left armhole steek, k2tog, k1, knit steek sts, k1, ssk, knit to end of round.

Repeat these decreases every other round 6 more times (7 times total)—152 sts on needle including steeks.

Work in pattern as established until 4 full repeats of chart 2 have been completed.

SHAPE NECK

Place a safety pin on each side of the front steek to indicate beginning of neck shaping. Continue working chart 2 as follows.

Next Round: K1, ssk, knit to 3 sts before neck steek, k2tog, k1. Repeat this decrease every other round 5 more times (6 times total)—140 sts on needle including steeks.

Continue in pattern as established until 5 full repeats of chart 2 have been completed, knit one row with black, then work rounds 1–3 of chart 1 once, decreasing 1 st on back on row 1—139 sts on needle. Keep the pattern continuous on each side of the armhole steeks—for example, if there are 2 white sts before the steek, knit 2 black sts after the steek and so on. Put all sts on holder.

STITCHING AND CUTTING

Machine stitch and cut the steek for the front opening, and both armholes. See page 129 for steek techniques.

SHOULDERS

Reserve 22 sts for each shoulder, front and back. Bind off shoulders together (see three-needle bind-off on page 127). Keep center 36 sts on holder for back neck.

FRONT BANDS

With larger 24" (60-cm) needle, black, and beginning at right front folding ridge, pick up by knitting 74 sts along right-front edge to safety pin. Turn and purl one row. Work rows 1–11 of chart 1. *Note:* Since you are working back and forth (not circularly) read the RS chart rows from right to left, and the WS chart rows from left to right.

Folding Ridge
With black, knit the next (WS) row.

Border Facing
Change to smaller 24" (60-cm) needle. With black and starting with a knit row, work 17 more rows of St st. Place sts on holder. Turn border facing to WS at folding ridge and tack down live sts to inside, covering cut edge of steek.

Work left-front band same as right-front band but begin at safety pin and pick up to folding ridge.

NECKBAND

With smaller 24" (60-cm) needle, black, and beginning at the point where right front border joins body, pick up by knitting 82 sts around the neck edge as follows: 23 sts up to shoulder, 36 from back-neck holder, 23 from shoulder to the point where left front border joins body. Turn and purl one row. *Note:* Since you are working back and forth (not circularly) read the RS chart rows from right to left, and the WS chart rows from left to right.

Work through row 6 of chart 1. With black, work 1 more row of St st, a knit row.

Folding Ridge
With black, knit the next (WS) row.

NECKBAND BORDER FACING

With black and starting with a knit row, work 10 more rows of St st. Place sts on string to hold. Turn border facing to WS at folding ridge and tack down live sts to inside, covering cut edge of steek.

ARMHOLE BANDS

The armhole bands are worked circularly with a facing. With smaller 16" (40-cm) needle, black yarn, and beginning at middle of underarm, pick up by knitting 112 sts around armhole including underarm sts. Join and work as follows.

Round 1: Purl.
Round 2: Knit.
Round 3: Purl (folding ridge).
Rounds 4–12: Knit (facing).

Place sts on string to hold. Turn facing to WS at folding ridge and tack down live sts to inside, covering the cut edge of the armhole steek.

FINISHING

Remove provisional cast on and tack down live sts to inside.
Weave in all ends. Wash and block.
Attach clasps to front borders.

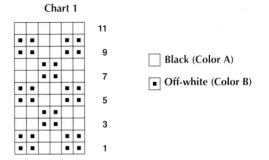

Chart 1

☐ Black (Color A)

▪ Off-white (Color B)

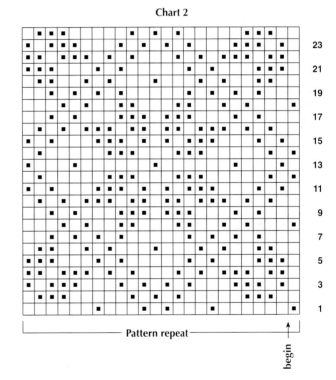

Chart 2

Pattern repeat

begin

Winter Sky

Winter Sky is based on photos of old Norwegian sweaters with simple patterns and decorative plackets at the neck. The double thickness of the placket that protects the vulnerable chest area makes Winter Sky especially warm and cozy.

Finished Sizes	Chest	Length
Size A	42½" (108 cm)	24" (61 cm)
Size B	45" (114.5 cm)	25½" (65 cm)
Size C	49½" (125.5 cm)	27" (68.5 cm)

Yarn: Rauma Strikkegarn (100% wool, 105 m [115 yd]/50 g [1.75 oz.]) color #104 Gray (Color A), 9 skeins; color #101 Off-white (Color B), 3 skeins.

Needles: 24" (60-cm) circular size 3 (3.25 mm) for A, size 4 (3.5 mm) for B, size 5 (3.75 mm) for C.

24" (60-cm) circular one size smaller than needle used for body. 24" (60-cm) and 16" (40-cm) circular needles two sizes smaller than needle used for body. Adjust needle size if necessary to obtain the correct gauge.

Notions: Stitch markers; stitch holders

Gauge in two-color pattern on larger needle
    Size A: 24 sts and 28 rows = 4" (10 cm)
    Size B: 22 sts and 26 rows = 4" (10 cm)
    Size C: 20 sts and 24 rows = 4" (10 cm)
    Remember: Gauge determines how your vest will fit. Swatch until you get it right.

Notes: The vest is worked circularly to the shoulders. Steeks are made for armholes and neck. (See page 129 for steek techniques.) Work in stockinette stitch using the two-color stranding technique, carrying the color not in use loosely across the back of the work. Do not carry the yarn over more than 5 sts without catching yarn in the back. (See page 128 for stranding techniques.)

BOTTOM BORDER
The border is worked in k2, p2 ribbing.
    With smaller 24" (60-cm) needle and color A, cast on 248 sts.
    Place a marker and join, being sure the sts are not twisted, by knitting into the first st on left needle. This st is the first st of each round and is the left underarm. Work k2, p2 ribbing for 2½" (6.5 cm).

BEGIN COLOR PATTERN
Next Round: Change to larger needle and begin chart 1. Mark right underarm by placing a marker

■ **Gray (Color A)**

□ **Off-white (Color B)**

Chart 1

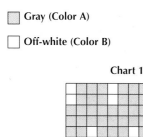

between the 123rd and 124th sts. Work the 8-round repeat 11 times, then work round 1 once more, ending 10 sts before left underarm marker.

RESERVE UNDERARM AND NECK STITCHES AND MAKE STEEKS

Next Round (round 2 of chart 1): Place next 21 sts on holder for left underarm. Place marker and cast on 5 sts using the backward loop method (see page 124). Place marker for end of steek. Work in pattern for 45 sts. Place next 33 sts on holder. Make a 5-st steek just like the first. Place marker for end of neck steek. Join again by knitting next st on left needle.

Work in pattern to 10 sts before right underarm marker. Place next 21 sts, including marker, on holder. Place marker and cast on 5 sts using the backward loop method. Place marker for end of right armhole steek. Join again by knitting into next stitch on left needle. Work to end of round—188 sts on needle including steeks.

Chart 2

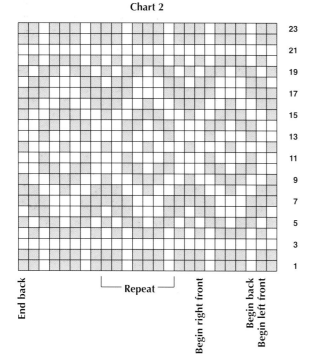

Chart 3

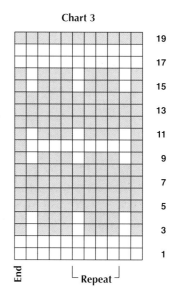

SHAPE ARMHOLE

Decreases for armhole shaping are worked on either side of each armhole steek. Remember to alternate colors on steek sts and keep the pattern as established.

Next Round (round 3 of chart 1): K1, ssk, work in pattern to 3 sts before right armhole steek, k2tog, k1, knit steek sts, k1, ssk. Work in pattern to 3 sts before left armhole steek, k2tog, k1, knit to end of round. Repeat these decreases every other round 9 more times (10 times total)—148 sts on needle including steeks.

Continue with chart 1 through round 6. On next round begin chart 2, making sure to start at indicated st for each front and the back. Complete chart 2.

SHAPE NECK

Change to chart 1 aligning first st over previous chart 1 pattern.

Decreases for neck shaping are worked on either side of the neck steek.

Next Round: Knit to 3 sts before neck steek, k2tog, k1, knit steek sts, k1, ssk, knit to end of round. Repeat these decreases every 6th round 2 more times (3 times total)—142 sts on needle.

Work 4 rounds even. Place all sts on holder.

STITCHING AND CUTTING

Machine stitch and cut steeks for front opening and armholes. (See page 129 for techniques.)

SHOULDERS

Reserve 22 sts for each shoulder, front and back. With wrong sides together, bind off shoulders together (see three-needle bind-off on page 127). Bind off the left shoulder from neck to shoulder, the right from shoulder to neck. Keep the center 39 sts on the holder for the back neck.

PLACKET

With larger needle, color A, and beginning on right front, pick up by knitting 45 sts to shoulder, knit 39 back neck sts, pick up by knitting 45 sts to bottom of placket—123 sts on needle. Turn and purl one row. Work chart 3. *Note:* You are working back and forth (not circularly)—read RS chart rows from right to left, WS chart rows from left to right. When chart 3 is complete, knit one WS row (folding ridge).

Placket Facing

Change to middle size needle and beginning with a knit row, work St st for 22 rows. Place all sts on holder.

Attach Placket to Front

Pick up by knitting 16 sts across bottom of each side of placket (patterned portion). With wrong sides together and using the three-needle bind-off (see page 127) bind off placket and front sts on holder together as follows: bind off 15 sts, bind off the next placket st with 2 sts from front holder, bind off 16 sts. Tack down live sts of facing to inside, covering cut edge.

ARMHOLE BANDS

The armhole bands are worked circularly with a facing.

With smaller 16" (40-cm) needle and color A, begin at the middle of underarm and pick up by knitting 100 sts around armhole including underarm sts. Join and purl one round (folding ridge). Knit 8 rounds. Place all sts on holder. Tack down live sts of facing to inside, covering cut edge.

FINISHING

Weave in all ends. Wash and block.

9

North America

The folklore of North America includes many superstitions concerning the proper wearing of clothes.
Accidentally putting a garment on inside out was considered by some to have special significance.
One little rhyme illustrates a common belief:

I don't know how it came about; I put my vest on wrong side out.
I could not change it back all day, for that would drive my luck away.

Dineh Blanket Vest

The Navajo call themselves Dineh, which means "the people." Navajo weaving began in the 1600s. By the 1800s, stripes and meanders, simple zigzag designs, had become traditional elements in their work. Weavers were able to add more color to their work by cutting up pieces of a Spanish cloth called bayeta, unraveling the yarn and using it in their own woven designs. A rich, rusty red was a favorite color.

The pattern of the Dineh Blanket Vest is based on the designs in a classic Navajo child's blanket in the Bert Lies collection.

Finished Sizes	Chest	Length
Size A	36" (91.5 cm)	21¾ (55 cm)
Size B	41½" (105.5 cm)	24½" (62 cm)
Size C	48¾" (124 cm)	27¾" (70.5 cm)

Yarn: Weaving Southwest Worsted Singles (100% wool, 190 yd [174 m]/4 oz [113 g]): Sangre (Color A), 4 skeins; Garnet (Color B) and Slate (Color C), 1 skein each.

Needles: Body needle: 24" (60-cm) circular size 6 (4 mm) for A, size 7 (4.5 mm) for B, size 8 (5 mm) for C. 24" (60-cm) and 16" (40-cm) circular needles two sizes smaller than needle used for body. 24" (60-cm) circular needle one size larger than needle used for body. Adjust needle size if necessary to obtain the correct gauge.

Notions: Five ⅝" (16 mm) buttons; stitch markers; stitch holders

Gauge in stockinette stitch on body needle
   Size A: 18 sts and 30 rows = 4" (10 cm)
   Size B: 16 sts and 26 rows = 4" (10 cm)
   Size C: 14 sts and 22 rows = 4" (10 cm)
   Remember: Gauge determines how your garment will fit. Swatch until you get it right.

Notes: Dineh is knitted in two pieces starting at the center back around to the front edges.

The vest is sized by gauge, changing needle size to change the size of the garment. It may also be enlarged by adding plain rows between the patterned rows on the chart. For example, size B has a row gauge of 6½ rows per inch, so adding six extra rows adds approximately an inch to the width of the body. Be sure to keep track and add the same number of rows in the same places on both sides of the vest.

RIGHT BACK

With 24" (60-cm) body needle and color B, use a provisional cast-on (see page 124) and cast on 94 sts. Follow chart through row 13. Change to larger needle for two-color pattern rows. Change back to body needle for plain stripes. (If you forget to change needles for a row or two it probably won't matter.) Continue to follow chart through row 44.

SHAPE ARMHOLE

Armhole Decreases
Next Row (RS): Work to last 40 sts, k2tog, k1, place last 37 sts on holder. Turn. (One decrease made.)
Row 1 (WS): Purl.
Row 2 (RS): Work to last 3 sts, k2tog, k1.
   Repeat rows 1 and 2 four more times (6 decreases total). Work even in pattern through row 66 of chart (mid-underarm).

RIGHT FRONT

Begin again at row 65. Work chart rows as before but in reverse order, i.e., 65, 64, 63, etc. for 10 rows.

Armhole Increases
Row 1 (RS): Work to last st, m1, k1.
Row 2 (WS): Purl.
   Repeat rows 1 and 2 four more times—56 sts on the needle.

Sangre (Color A)

Garnet (Color B)

Slate (Color C)

Next Row: Work to last st, m1, k1, cast-on 37 sts—
94 sts on needle

SHAPE NECK

Beginning on row 22 (WS), bind off 4 sts at beginning
of this and every other row 10 times. Complete chart.
Place right-front sts on holder.

LEFT BACK

With 24" (60-cm) body needle and color B, use a provisional cast-on and cast on 94 sts. Follow chart through
row 13. Change to larger needle for two-color pattern
rows. Change back to body needle for plain stripes. (If
you forget to change needles for a row or two it probably won't matter.) Follow chart through row 44.

SHAPE ARMHOLE

Armhole Decreases

Next Row (RS): Work 37 sts and put them on holder.
    K1, k2tog, work to end. Turn. (One decrease
    made.)

Row 1 (WS): Purl.

Row 2 (RS): K1, k2tog, knit to end.
    Repeat decrease rows 1 and 2 four more times.
    Work even in pattern through row 66 of chart (mid-
underarm).

LEFT FRONT

Begin again at row 65. Work chart rows as before
but in reverse order, i.e., 65, 64, 63, etc. for 10 rows.

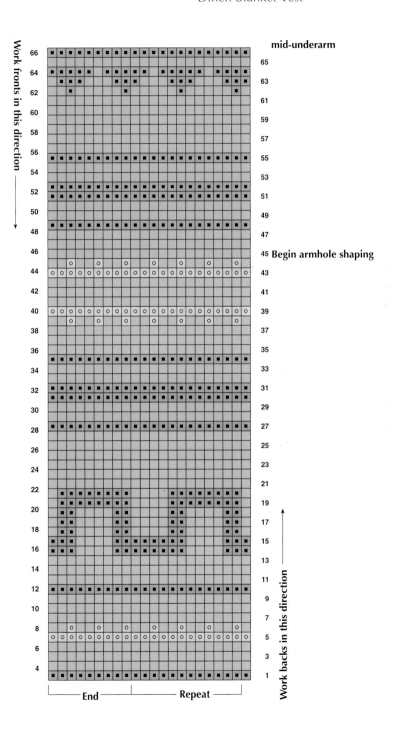

Armhole Increases
Row 1 (RS): K1, m1, work to end.
Row 2 (WS): Purl.
   Repeat rows 1 and 2 four more times—56 sts on needle. Break yarn.
Next Row (RS): Using long-tail cast-on and color A, cast on 37 sts on right needle, k1 from left needle, m1, work to end.
Next Row: Purl in pattern to end. 94 sts on needle.

SHAPE NECK
Beginning on row 21 (RS) bind off 4 sts at beginning of this and every other row 10 times. Complete chart. Place left-front sts on holder.

SHOULDERS
With right sides together, sew shoulders together.

JOIN AT CENTER BACK
Place the center back right and center back left sts on separate needles. With right sides together, bind off backs together (see three-needle bind-off on page 127).

BOTTOM BORDER
With smallest 24" needle and color A, pick up by knitting 175 sts along bottom edge. Knit 6 rows. Bind off.

FRONT AND NECK BORDERS
With smallest 24" (60-cm) needle and beginning at bottom of right front, pick up by knitting 58 sts to the beginning of V neck, 60 sts to center back, 60 sts to V neck, and 58 sts to bottom of left front—236 sts on needle. Knit 3 rows.

Buttonholes (Women's Version)
Next Row (RS): K4, yo, k2tog, *k10, yo, k2tog; repeat from * 3 more times, knit to end.

Buttonholes (Men's Version)
Next Row (RS): K182, k2tog, yo, *k10, k2tog, yo; repeat from * 3 more times, end k4.

Knit 6 rows. Bind off loosely.

ARMHOLE BORDERS
Right Armhole
With 16" (40-cm) needle and beginning at middle of underarm, pick up by knitting 13 sts to holder, k37 from holder, pick up by knitting 50 sts to middle of underarm—100 sts on needle. Join. Purl 1 round, purling 4tog at shoulder seam, knit 1 round. Bind off in purl.

Left Armhole
With 16" (40-cm) needle and beginning at middle of underarm, pick up by knitting 50 sts to shoulder, k37 from holder, pick up by knitting 13 sts to middle of underarm—100 sts on needle. Join. Purl 1 round, purling 4tog at shoulder seam, knit 1 round. Bind off in purl.

FINISHING
Weave in all ends. Wash and block.
Sew buttons along front edge opposite buttonholes.

Bookworm Vest

Contemporary American folklore is often found in the movies. The movie *Funny Face* is a modern version of the Cinderella story. A charming little bookworm works as a clerk in a secondhand bookstore in Greenwich Village. Her life changes completely when she is accidentally "discovered" and transformed (lovely creature that she is) by the world of high fashion. Swept away to her dream city, Paris, she finds both enlightenment and love. The Bookworm vest was inspired by the little clerk's simple and practical working wear.

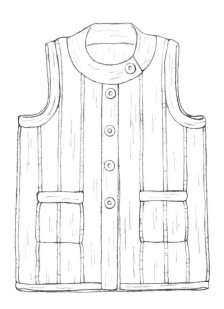

Finished Sizes	Chest	Length
Size A	44" (112 cm)	30" (76 cm)
Size B	48" (122 cm)	31" (79 cm)
Size C	52" (132 cm)	31" (79 cm)

Yarn: Reynolds Turnberry Tweed (100% wool, 220 yd [210 m]/100 g [3.5 oz]): Color #027 Charcoal tweed, 4 (4, 5) skeins

Needles: 24" (60-cm) circular size 7 (4.5 mm). 24" (60-cm) and 16" (40-cm) circular needles two sizes smaller than needle used for body.

Notions: Five 1½" (4 cm) buttons, stitch markers, scrap yarn, stitch holders

Gauge in stockinette stitch
18 sts and 26 rows = 4" (10 cm)
Remember: Gauge determines how your garment will fit. Swatch until you get it right.

Note: The vest is knitted in one piece to the underarms and then the fronts and back are worked separately.

PATTERN STITCH
Row 1 (RS): K10 (11, 12), p2, *k9 (10, 11), p2; repeat from * to last 10 (11, 12) sts, knit to end.
Row 2 (WS): Purl.
Repeat rows 1 and 2 for pattern.

BODY
With smaller 24" (60-cm) needle and using a long-tail cast-on (see page 123) cast on 187 (204, 221) sts.
Place a marker between the 45th (49th, 53rd) and 46th (50th, 54th) sts and between the 142nd (155th, 168th) and 143rd (156th, 169th) sts. Work in garter st for 8 rows.
Next Row (RS): Change to larger needle and begin pattern stitch.

Repeat pattern stitch until piece measures 11½ (12, 12)" (29 [30.5, 30.5] cm) from cast-on edge, ending with a WS row.

RESERVE POCKET OPENING
Next Row (RS): Work 10 (11, 12) sts in pattern; knit next 24 (26, 28) sts with contrasting scrap yarn. Turn and knit the same sts again with the scrap yarn. Turn and, with vest yarn, knit the 24 (26, 28) pocket sts again; continue in pattern to last 34 (37, 40) sts. Work second pocket opening as for first, end knit 10 (11, 12) sts.

Continue in pattern until piece measures 20 (20½, 20½)" (51 [52, 52] cm) from cast-on edge, ending with a WS row.

DIVIDE FOR UNDERARMS/RESERVE UNDERARM AND FRONT STITCHES
Next Row (RS): Work in pattern as established to 10 (11, 12) sts past first marker and place last 22 (24, 26) sts worked (including marker) on holder for right underarm. Work to 12 (11, 10) sts past second marker and place last 22 (24, 26) sts worked (including marker) on holder for left underarm. Work to end of row, break off yarn, and place both fronts on holders, leaving only the center 77 (84, 91) sts on needle for back. With WS facing, join yarn and work one row.

BACK
Shape Armholes
Next Row (RS): K1, ssk, work in pattern as established to last 3 sts, k2tog, k1. Repeat this shaping every other row 8 more times (9 times total)—59 (66, 73) sts on needle. Work in pattern until armhole measures 10 (10½, 10½)" (25.5 [26.5, 26.5] cm) from underarm. Place back sts on holder.

LEFT FRONT
Place left-front stitches on needle. Attach yarn at neck edge and work one WS row.

Shape Armhole
Next Row (RS): K1, ssk, work in pattern as established to end. Repeat this armhole shaping every other row 8 more times (9 times total)—24 (27, 30) sts on needle. Work in pattern until armhole measures 5" (12.5 cm) from underarm, ending with a RS row. Break yarn. Turn.

Shape Neck
Next Row (WS): Place first 11 (12, 13) sts on holder, attach yarn and finish the WS row.
Decrease Row (RS): Work in pattern to last 3 sts, k2 tog, k1. Work this decrease every other row 4 more times (5 times total)—8 (10, 12) shoulder sts left on needle. Continue in pattern on remaining sts until front measures same as back. Place left-front sts on a holder.

RIGHT FRONT
Place right-front sts on needle. Attach yarn at armhole edge and work one WS row.

Shape Armhole
Next Row (RS): Work in pattern to last 3 sts, k2tog, k1. Repeat this shaping every other row 8 more times (9 times total)—24 (27, 30) sts on needle. Work in pattern until armhole measures 5" (12.5 cm) from underarm, ending with a WS row. Break yarn.

Shape Neck
Next Row (RS): Place first 11 (12, 13) sts on holder, join yarn, work in pattern to end. Turn and work back.

Decrease Row (RS): K1, ssk, work in pattern to end. Work this decrease every other row 4 more times—8 (10, 12) shoulder sts left on needle. Continue in pattern on remaining sts until front measures the same as back. Place right-front sts on holder.

POCKETS

Remove scrap yarn from pocket opening and with larger needle pick up 24 (26, 28) top sts and with smaller needle pick up 24 (26, 28) bottom sts.

Top sts become the pocket lining. Work in St st for 5" (12.5 cm). Bind off.

Bottom sts become the pocket border. Work in garter st for 12 rows. Bind off.

SHOULDERS

Bind off shoulder seams together (see three-needle bind-off on page 127).

FRONT/NECKBANDS

Buttonhole Band

With smaller 24" (60-cm) needle and beginning at bottom of right front, pick up by knitting 79 (84, 84) sts. Work in garter st for 19 rows.

Buttonholes

Row 1 (RS): Knit 31 (36, 36), *bind off 4, k9, repeat from * 3 more times, ending last repeat k5.

Row 2 (WS): *Knit to next buttonhole, cast on 4 sts; repeat from *, end by knitting to end of row.

Row 3: Knit to end, knitting into the back of the st after each buttonhole to tighten it.
Knit 10 more rows. Bind off.

Buttonband

With smaller 24" (60-cm) needle and beginning at top of left front, pick up by knitting 79 (84, 84) sts. Work in garter st for 22 rows. Bind off.

Neckband

With smaller 24" (60-cm) needle, RS facing, and beginning at right front edge, pick up by knitting 121 (126, 129) sts around neck as follows: pick up 12 sts across front border, 11 (12, 12) sts from holder, 16 sts to shoulder, 43 (46, 49) back neck sts, 16 sts to holder, 11 (12, 12) sts from holder, 12 sts across front border. Turn and knit one row, casting on 13 sts at end of row. Knit 10 more rows. Bind off.

ARMHOLE BANDS

Bands are worked circularly. With 16" (40-cm) needle and beginning at middle of the underarm, pick up by knitting 88 (93, 93) sts around armhole including underarm sts. Join and work in circular garter st (purl 1 round, knit 1 round) for 8 rounds. Bind off.

FINISHING

Sew down pocket linings and bands.
Weave in all ends. Wash and block.
Sew buttons opposite buttonholes.

10

Switzerland

The Swiss Village Museum in New Glarus, Wisconsin, provides a wealth of information on the pioneer lives of Swiss settlers who came to America in the nineteenth century. From cheese making and beekeeping to lace making, the skills and talents of the Swiss immigrants are displayed. Traditional costumes are worn at the festivals that are held throughout the year. One women's costume includes beautifully knitted lace scarves worn as collars over traditional bodices. The lace collar vest was inspired by this costume.

Swiss Collar Vest

Finished Sizes	Chest	Length
Size A	38" (96.5 cm)	21½" (54.5 cm)
Size B	42" (106.5 cm)	22" (56 cm)
Size C	48" (122 cm)	24½" (62 cm)

Yarn: Jamieson and Smith's 2-ply (100% wool [150 yd (137 m)/25 g (1 oz.)]): color #55 Red, #7 (8, 9) skeins; color #1A Cream, 1 skein.

Needles: 24" (60-cm) circular size 3 (3.25 mm) for vest; 24" (60-cm) and 16" (40-cm) circular needles one size smaller than needle used for vest; 24" (60-cm) circular size 7 (4.5 mm) for collar. Adjust needle sizes if necessary to obtain the correct gauges.

Notions: Seven ½" (12 mm) buttons; 2 safety pins; stitch markers; stitch holders

Gauge in stockinette stitch on larger needle
  Vest: 24 sts and 34 rows = 4" (10 cm)
  Collar: 14–16 sts = 4" (10 cm) (blocked and
  stretched)
  Remember: Gauge determines how your garment
will fit. Swatch until you get it right.

Notes: Vest is worked in one piece to underarm. Fronts
and back are then worked separately to shoulders.
Using smaller needles at the waist gives vest a slightly
tapered shape. The collar is not attached and this classic vest can be worn on its own.

BACK AND FRONTS

With smaller 24" (60-cm) needle cast on 222 (246,
282) sts. Place marker between 55th (60th, 70th) st and
56th (61st, 71st) sts and between 167th (186th, 212th)
and 168th (187th, 213th) sts. Work garter st (knit every
row) for 1 inch ending with a WS row.

Change to larger 24" (60-cm) needle and work in
St st until piece measures 3½ (4, 5)" (9 [10, 20.5] cm)
from cast-on edge.
  Change to smaller 24" (60-cm) needle and work in
St st until piece measures 6½ (7, 8)" (16.5 [18, 20.5]
cm) from cast-on edge.
  Change to larger 24" (60-cm) needle and work in
St st until piece measures 11½ (12½, 13½)" (29 [31.5,
34.5] cm) from cast-on edge, ending with a WS row.

DIVIDE FOR UNDERARMS/RESERVE UNDERARMS AND FRONTS

Next Row (RS): Knit to 13 (14, 16) sts past first
  marker, place the last 26 (28, 32) sts worked
  (including marker) on holder for right underarm.
  Work to 13 (14, 16) sts past second marker and
  place the last 26 (28, 32) sts worked (including
  marker) on holder for left underarm. Work to end
  of row, break off yarn, and place both fronts on
  holders, leaving only center 86 (98, 110) sts on
  needle for back. Turn, join yarn, and work one
  (WS) row.

BACK

Shape Armholes

Next Row (RS): Work in pattern as established and
  decrease 1 st at each armhole edge as follows:
  K1, ssk, work in pattern as established to last 3
  sts, k2tog, k1. Repeat this shaping every other
  row 7 (9, 11) more times (8 [10, 12] times total).
  Work even until armhole measures 9½ (10, 10½)"
  (24 [25.5, 26.5] cm) from underarm, ending with
  a RS row.

Shape Shoulders

Shoulders are shaped with short rows as follows (see
page 126 for short-row techniques):

Set 1: On next WS row *work to last 4 (4, 6) sts, slip and wrap next st, turn and repeat from * once. Turn.

Set 2: On next WS row *work to last 7 (7, 10) sts, slip and wrap next st, turn and repeat from * once. Turn.

Set 3: On next WS row *work to last 10 (10, 14) sts, slip and wrap next st, turn and repeat from * once. Turn.

Next Row (WS): Purl, hiding the wraps. Place back sts on holder.

LEFT FRONT

Shape Armhole

Place left-front sts on needle. Attach yarn at neck edge and work one WS row.

Next Row (RS): K1, ssk, knit to end.

Repeat armhole shaping every other row 7 (9, 11) more times (8 [10, 12] times total). Purl one row.

Shape Neck

Next Row (RS): Knit to last 3 sts, k2tog, k1. Repeat this decrease alternating every other and then every 4th row 9 (10, 11) more times—14 (14, 18) sts on the needle, ending on RS row.

Shape Shoulder

Set 1: On next row (WS) work to last 4 (4, 6) sts, wrap and turn, work to end.

Set 2: Work to last 7 (7, 10) sts, wrap and turn, work to end.

Set 3: Work to last 10 (10, 14) sts, wrap and turn, work to end.

Next Row (WS): Purl, hiding the wraps. Place sts on holder.

RIGHT FRONT

Shape Armhole

Place right-front sts on needle. Attach yarn at armhole edge and work one WS row.

Next Row (RS): Knit to last 3 sts, k2tog, k1 (armhole shaping). Repeat the armhole shaping decrease every other row 7 (9, 11) more times (8 [10, 12] times total).

Shape Neck

Next Row: K1, ssk, knit to end of row. Repeat this decrease alternating every other and then every 4th row 9 (10, 11) more times—14 (14, 18) sts on needle. Work one WS row.

Shape Shoulder

Set 1: On next (RS) row work to last 4 (4, 6) sts, wrap and turn, work to end.

Set 2: Work to last 7 (7, 10) sts, wrap and turn, work to end.

Set 3: Work to last 10 (10, 14) sts, wrap and turn, work to end.

Next Row (RS): Purl, hiding the wraps. Place sts on holder.

SHOULDERS

With right sides held together, bind off shoulders together (see three-needle bind-off on page 127).

BUTTON, BUTTONHOLE, AND NECKBANDS

Front and neckbands are worked in one piece in garter stitch. Place safety pins at the beginning of the V neck shaping on each front. With smaller 24" (60-cm) needle begin at bottom of right front and pick up by knitting 62 (68, 75) sts to safety pin, 44 (49, 56) sts to shoulder, 42 (50, 50) back neck sts, 44 (49, 56) sts to next safety pin and 62 (68, 75) sts from pin to bottom of left front—254 (284, 312) sts on needle. Work in garter st for 5 rows.

Buttonholes

Next Row (RS): Knit 2 (2, 3), k2tog, (yo) twice, *k9 (10, 11), k2tog, (yo) twice; repeat from * 5 more times, knit to end.

Next Row (WS): Knit, working double yarnovers as one st (drop extra loop of double yarnover). Knit 5 more rows. Bind off in knit.

ARMHOLE BANDS

Armhole bands are worked circularly in garter st (purl 1 row, knit 1 row). With 16" (40-cm) needle and beginning at middle of underarm holder, pick up by knitting 113 (125, 143) sts around armhole including underarm sts. Join and alternate purl rounds and knit rounds for 6 rounds. Bind off in knit.

FINISHING

Weave in all ends. Wash and block.
Sew buttons opposite buttonholes.

COLLAR

Collar is worked from top to bottom. Cast on 5 sts.
Row 1: K1, yo, k1, yo, k1 (mark this as center st), yo, k1, yo, k1—9 sts.
Row 2: P1, m1, purl to last st, m1, p1—11 sts.
Row 3: K1, yo, knit to center st, yo, k1, yo, knit to the last st, yo, k1—15 sts.
Row 4: Repeat row 2—17 sts.
Row 5: K1, yo, k1, *yo, k2tog, repeat from * to center st, yo, k1 (center st), *yo, k2tog; repeat from * to last 2 sts, yo, k1, yo, k1—21 sts.
Row 6: Repeat row 2—23 sts.
Row 7: K1, yo, k1, *yo, k2tog; repeat from * to one st before center st, yo, k1, yo, k1 (center st), yo, k1, *yo, k2 tog; repeat from * to last 2 sts, yo, k1, yo, k1.
Row 8: Repeat row 2.
Repeat rows 7 and 8 for pattern 20 (20, 24) more times. Knit 4 rows, repeating increases as established. Knit 4 rows without increases. Bind off loosely. Weave in all ends. Wash and block.

11

China

According to folk belief in China, the fortunate home is adopted by chi spirits. Considered to be pure energy, chi spirits are invited to move freely around the house. Their uninhibited movement is considered very beneficial to the inhabitants, increasing stamina, improving health, and giving protection to the home. Furniture is placed so that it will not interfere with the flow of energy, and mirrors are used as portals for chi spirits to pass through otherwise-confining walls of the home.

Chinese Red Vest

The color red is well-loved in China. Chinese parents often sew bits of red cloth into the pockets of their children's clothes to protect them from evil spirits. In the practice of Feng Shui, the Chinese art of environmental design, red represents happiness and strength.

Finished Sizes	Chest	Length
Size A	42" (107 cm)	21½" (54.5 cm)
Size B	46" (117 cm)	23" (58.5 cm)
Size C	50" (127 cm)	24½" (62 cm)

Yarn: Rauma Strikkegarn (100% wool; 105 m [115 yd]/50 g [1.75 oz.]): color #144 Red, 7 (8, 9) skeins

Needles: 24" (60-cm) circular size 4 (3.5 mm). 24" (60-cm) and 16" (40-cm) circular needles one size smaller than needle used for body. Adjust needle size if necessary to obtain the correct gauge.

Notions: Seven ³⁄₈" (10 mm) shank buttons; stitch markers; stitch holders

Gauge in stockinette stitch on larger needle
20 sts and 28 rows = 4" (10 cm)
Remember: Gauge determines how your garment will fit. Swatch until you get it right.

Notes: Button loops are made as the front edge is bound off. Button loops are on the "men's" side only as is traditional. Neck border is worked with shaping decreases like a yoke sweater.

SEED STITCH
Row 1: *K1, p1; repeat from *, end k1.
   Repeat row 1 for pattern.

BORDER PATTERN: (Row 1 is a WS row)
Rows 1–6: Knit (garter st).
Rows 7–13: Work in seed st.
Rows 14–19: Knit (garter st).

MAIN PATTERN (Row 1 is a RS row)
Row 1: Knit.

Rows 2, 4, and 6: Purl.
Row 3: K1, *p1, k3; repeat from *, end last repeat k1.
Row 5: Knit
Row 7: *K3, p1; repeat from * to last 3 sts, k3.
Row 8: Purl.

BACK AND FRONTS
Vest is worked in one piece to underarm.

With larger needle, cast on 195 (215, 235) sts. Work row 1 of Border Pattern, placing markers between the 45th (49th, 54th) and 46th (50th, 55th) sts and between the 150th (166th, 181st) and 151st (167th, 182nd) sts to mark sides. Complete Border Pattern. Begin Main Pattern. Repeat Main Pattern until piece measures 10 (11, 12)" (25.5 [28, 30.5] cm) from cast-on edge, ending with a RS row.

DIVIDE FOR UNDERARMS/RESERVE UNDERARMS AND FRONTS
Next Row (WS): Work in pattern as established to 1 (2, 2) sts past first marker, place last 2 (4, 4) sts worked (including marker) on holder for left underarm. Work to 1 (2, 2) sts past second marker and place last 2 (4, 4) sts worked (including marker) on holder for right underarm. Work to end of row, break off yarn, and place both fronts on holders, leaving only the center 103 (113, 123) sts on needle for back.

BACK
Shape Armholes
Next Row (RS): Work in pattern as established and decrease 1 st at each armhole edge as follows: K1, ssk, work in pattern as established to last 3 sts, k2 tog, k1. Repeat this shaping every other row 14 (17, 19) more times [15 (18, 20) times total]—73 (77, 83) sts on needle. Work even in

pattern until back measures 10½ (11, 11½)" (26.5 [28, 29]cm) from underarm, ending with a WS row.

Back Neck Shaping
Next Row: Work pattern for 12 (13, 15) sts, place center 49 (51, 53) sts on holder, place remaining 12 (13, 15) sts on separate holder. Left and right back are worked separately. Turn and work a WS row on the right-back sts.

Right Back
Next Row (RS): Work in pattern to last 3 sts, k2tog, k1. Work this decrease every other row once more. Work in pattern until armhole measures 12 (12½, 13)" (30.5 [31.5, 33] cm) from underarm ending on WS row. Place right-back sts on holder.

Left Back
Place the left-back sts on needle. Beginning with a RS row, work 2 rows in pattern.
Next Row (RS): K1, ssk, work in pattern to end. Work this decrease row every other row once more. Work in pattern until armhole measures 12 (12½, 13)" (30.5 [31.5, 33] cm) from underarm ending on WS row. Place left-back sts on holder.

LEFT FRONT
Place the left-front sts on needle.

Shape Armhole
Next Row (RS): K1, ssk, work in pattern as established to end. Repeat this shaping every other row 14 (17, 19) more times [15 (18, 20) times total]—29 (29, 32) sts on needle. Work in pattern until armhole measures 7 (7½, 8)" (18, [19, 20.5] cm) from underarm, ending with a WS row.

Shape Neck
Next Row (RS): Work in pattern to last 8 (8, 10) sts and put them on holder. Turn and work back.
Decrease Row (RS): Work in pattern to last 3 sts, k2tog, k1. Work this decrease every other row 10 (9, 8) more times (11 [10, 9]) times total—10 (11, 13) sts on needle. Continue in pattern on remaining sts until front has same number of rows as back ending on WS row. Place left-front sts on holder.

RIGHT FRONT
Place the right-front sts on needle.

Shape Armhole
Next Row (RS): Work in pattern as established to last 3 sts, k2tog, k1. Repeat this shaping every other row 14 (17, 19) more times [15 (18, 20) times total]—29 (29, 32) sts on needle. Work in pattern until armhole measures 7 (7½, 8)" (18, [19, 20.5] cm) from underarm, ending with a WS row 8 (8, 10) sts before end of row. Place these 8 (8, 10) sts on holder.

Shape Neck
Next Row (RS): Work in pattern to end. Turn and work back.
Decrease Row (RS): K1, ssk, work in pattern to end. Work this decrease every other row 10 (9, 8) more times (11 [10, 9]) times total—10 (11, 13) sts on needle. Continue in pattern on remaining sts until front has same number of rows as back ending on WS row. Place right-front sts on holder.

FINISHING
Shoulders
With right sides together, bind off shoulders together (see three-needle bind-off on page 127).

FRONT BORDERS

Right Front: With smaller needle, RS facing, and beginning at bottom of right front, pick up by knitting 92 (97, 102) sts. Turn and work border pattern through row 18. Bind off in knit.

Left Front: With smaller needle, RS facing, and beginning at top of left front, pick up by knitting 92 (97, 102) sts. Turn and work border pattern through row 18.

Button Loops

Next Row (WS): Binding off in knit, bind off 41 sts, *(yo, bind off 1 st) 3 times, bind off 10 (11, 12) sts; repeat from * 4 more times, (yo, bind off 1 st) 3 times, bind off 1 st.

NECK BORDER

With smaller needle, RS facing, and beginning at top of the right front border, pick up by knitting 10 sts across border, 8 (8, 10) sts from front neck holder, 24 sts to shoulder, 10 sts to back neck, 49 (51, 53) sts from back neck holder, 10 sts to shoulder, 24 sts from shoulder, 8 (8, 10) sts from front neck holder, and 10 sts across left-front border—153 (155, 161) sts on needle. Turn and work rows 1–5 of Border Pattern.

Next Row (row 6 of border pattern): Decrease 10 (11, 11) sts evenly spaced—143 (144, 150) sts on needle. Work rows 7–13 of border pattern.

Next Row (row 14 of border pattern): Decrease 12 (13, 13) sts evenly spaced—131 (131, 137) sts on needle. Complete border pattern through row 18.

Next Row (WS): Binding off in knit, k1, (yo, bind off 1 st) 3 times (button loop made), bind off to end.

COLLAR

With smaller needle and beginning 5 sts in from right-front edge, pick up by knitting 81 (83, 85) sts, ending 5 sts short of left-front edge. Work rows 1–9 of border pattern. Work rows 14–18, decreasing 1 st at each neck edge every row. Bind off in knit.

ARMHOLE BORDERS

Armhole borders are knitted circularly.

With 16" (40-cm) needle, RS facing, and beginning at middle of underarm sts on holder, pick up by knitting 120 (124, 128) sts around armhole including underarm sts. Join and purl one round. Bind off in knit.

FINISHING

Weave in all ends. Wash and block.
Sew buttons opposite button loops.

12

England

The folklore of Britain has many stories about fairies and their deeds. Fairies are known to be both of great benefit to humans and also to be able to cause untold problems for the unfortunate human who offends them. One such story claims that a spinner must never leave the tension on the band of her spinning wheel at the end of the day lest the fairies use it to spin during the night. This warning seems strange at first, since having a good fairy to help with the spinning sounds like a good idea. As the story goes, the drawback is that if the fairy spinner should ever become cross with her human counterpart, she may leave and take all her spinning with her, even if it has already been knitted into a garment. Offend your good fairy and you could literally lose the sweater off your back!

British School Slipover

Traditional clothing for English schoolchildren often includes a knitted vest, usually of a neutral color and frequently with a school badge or crest.

Finished Sizes	Chest	Length
Size A	39" (99 cm)	25½" (65 cm)
Size B	43" (109 cm)	26" (66 cm)
Size C	48" (122 cm)	26½" (67.5 cm)

Yarn: Rowan Wool Cotton (50% merino, 50% cotton, 123 yd [113 m]/50g): Color #903 Gray, 8 (8, 9) balls.

Needles: 24" (60-cm) circular needle size 5 (3.75 mm). 24" (60-cm) and 16" (40-cm) circular needle two sizes smaller than needle used for body. Adjust needle size if necessary to obtain the correct gauge.

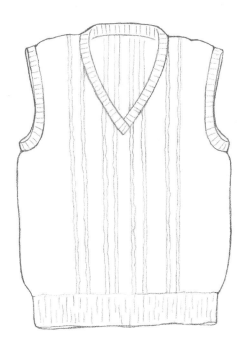

Notions: Stitch markers; stitch holder; cable needle

Gauge in stockinette stitch on larger needle
  20 stitches and 28 rows = 4" (10 cm)
  Remember: Gauge determines how your garment will fit. Swatch until you get it right.

Note: The vest is worked circularly up to the under-arms and then divided to work the back and front separately.

BOTTOM BORDER

With smaller 24" (60-cm) needle cast on 208 (228, 248) sts. Being careful not to twist sts, place marker and join into a round by knitting into the first st on left nee-dle. This st is the first st of each round and marks the left underarm. Work in k1, p1 ribbing for 3" (7.5 cm).
Next Round: Change to larger needle. K27 (32, 37), work round 1 of chart, k27 (32, 37), pm for right

underarm, k27 (32, 37), work round 1 of chart, k27 (32, 37).
  Continue working pattern as established until body measures 11½ (11½, 12½)" (29 [29, 32] cm) above rib-bing. End with an odd-numbered round, 8 (11, 14) sts before left underarm marker.

RESERVE UNDERARM STITCHES

Place next 16 (22, 28) sts on holder for left underarm; place next 88 (92, 96) sts on holder for front; place next 16 (22, 28) sts on holder for right underarm—88 (92, 96) sts remain for back.

BACK

Next Row (WS): Keeping pattern as established, turn and work one row (an even-numbered row) of back—88 (92, 96) sts on needle. *Note:* The knit-ting is now back and forth, not circular. Read the even-numbered (WS) rows of chart from left to right and the odd-numbered (RS) rows from right to left.

SHAPE ARMHOLE

Next Row (RS): K1, ssk, work in pattern to last 3 sts, k2tog, k1.
  Repeat these decreases every other row 6 (6, 7) more times (7 [7, 8] times total)—74 (78, 80) sts left on needle.
  Work in established pattern until back measures 10½ (11½, 11½)" (26.5 [29, 29] cm) from underarm. Place all sts on holder.

FRONT

Join yarn, keep pattern as established, and beginning with a WS (even-numbered) row, work as for back until armhole shaping is complete, ending with a WS (even-numbered) row.
Next Row (RS): Work in pattern for 37 (39, 40) sts.
  Place next 37 (39, 40) sts on holder for right front.

Left Front

Turn and work back in pattern.

Next Row (RS): Work to last 3 sts, k2tog, k1. Repeat this decrease row alternating every other and then every 4th row 6 more times (13 decreases), then every 4th row 6 (7, 7) more times—18 (19, 20) sts on needle. Work even until armhole measures same as for back. Place sts on holder.

Right Front

Place 37 (39, 40) sts on needle, attach yarn, and keeping pattern as established, begin at neck edge with a RS row.

Next Row (RS): K1, ssk, work in pattern to end. Repeat this decrease row alternating every other and then every 4th row 6 more times (13 decreases), then every 4th row 6 (7, 7) more times—18 (19, 20) sts on needle. Work even until armhole measures same as for back.

SHOULDERS

Reserve 18 (19, 20) sts for each shoulder, front and back. Bind off shoulders together (see three-needle bind-off

on page 127). Keep center 38 (40, 40) sts on holder for back neck.

NECKBAND

With smaller needle, and beginning at bottom of right front, pick up by knitting 48 (49, 49) sts to shoulder, knit 38 (40, 40) back neck sts decreasing 2 sts evenly spaced, pick up by knitting 48 (49, 49) sts to bottom of left front—132 (136, 136) sts. Turn and work k1, p1 ribbing for 10 rows. Bind off in ribbing. Cross right-front ribbing over top of left-front ribbing and sew into place.

ARMHOLE BANDS

Armhole bands are worked circularly. With smaller needle, and beginning at middle of underarm, pick up by knitting 118 (128, 134) sts around armhole including the underarm sts. Join and work k1, p1 ribbing for 10 rounds. Bind off in ribbing.

FINISHING

Weave in all ends. Wash and block.

☐   **knit on RS; purl WS**

▪   **purl on RS; knit on WS**

⧖   **2/2 Right Cross: place 2 sts on cn to back, k2, k2 from cn**

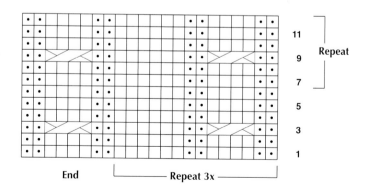

Prince of Wales Slipover

The pattern of the Prince of Wales Slipover is based on the Fair Isle sweater worn in a famous portrait of HRH The Prince of Wales by John St. Heiler Lander. This publicity caused Fair Isle sweaters to become all the rage for fashion mavens of the 1920s. According to experts who have seen the real sweater, the artist took some license with the design and color, but it makes a lovely garment nonetheless.

Finished Sizes	Chest	Length
Size A	41½" (105.5 cm)	24¼" (61.5 cm)
Size B	44½" (113 cm)	25½" (65 cm)
Size C	48" (122 cm)	27" (68.5 cm)

Yarn: Jamieson's 2-ply Shetland (100% Shetland wool [150 yd [137 m]/25 g])
Color A (#106 Mooskit), 4 skeins
Color B (#524 Poppy), 2 skeins
Color C (#80 Dark Green), 2 skeins
Color D (#788 Leaf), 2 skeins
Color E (#198 Peat), 2 skeins
Color F (#187 Sunrise), 2 skeins
Color G (#1160 Scotch Broom), 2 skeins

Needles: 24" (60-cm) circular size 2 (3 mm) for A, size 3 (3.25 mm) for B, size 4 (3.5 mm) for C. 24" (60-cm) and 16" (40-cm) circular needles two sizes smaller than needle used for body. Adjust needle size if necessary to obtain the correct gauge.

Notions: Stitch markers; stitch holders

Gauge in Fair Isle pattern on larger needle (see page 128 for two-color swatching instructions).

Size A: 30 stitches and 34 rows = 4" (10 cm)
Size B: 28 stitches and 32 rows = 4" (10 cm)
Size C: 26 stitches and 30 rows = 4" (10 cm)
Remember: Gauge determines how your garment will fit. Swatch until you get it right.

The slipover is worked circularly up to the shoulders. Steeks are made for armholes and neck opening (see page 129 for an explanation of steeks). Work in St st using two-color stranding technique, carrying color not in use loosely across back of work.

BOTTOM BORDER

Border is worked in corrugated ribbing. With smaller 24" (60-cm) needle and color A, cast on 296 sts. Place marker at beginning of round. This is the left underarm marker. Being careful not to twist sts, join into a round by knitting into the first st on left needle. This st is the first st of each round. With color A, work one round of k2, p2 ribbing.

Next Round: Begin to work corrugated ribbing in the following color sequence:

Rounds 1–4: K2 A, p2 C.
Rounds 5–14: K2 A, p2 D.
Rounds 15–18: K2 A, p2 C.
Next Round: Change to larger needle and knit with color A, increasing 16 sts evenly spaced (alternating every 18th and 19th st)—312 sts on needle.
Next Round: Knit with color A and place marker between 156th and 157th sts for right underarm.

BEGIN COLOR PATTERN

Note: To accommodate the stitch multiples of chart A and chart B, 4 sts must be decreased before chart B (to 308 sts) and increased (back to 312 sts) before chart A

is begun again. Increase or decrease at the center of both front and back and on each side as follows:

Decrease Round (round 23 of chart A): With color A, *k76, k2tog, repeat from * 3 more times (308 sts on the needle).

Increase Round (round 13 of chart B): With color E *k77, M1, repeat from * 3 more times (312 sts on the needle).

*Work chart A, decreasing 4 sts evenly spaced in last round—308 sts on needle—then chart B, increasing 4 sts evenly spaced on last round—312 sts on needle. Repeat from * once then work rounds 1–17 of chart A, ending 15 sts before left underarm marker.

RESERVE UNDERARM STITCHES

Next Round (round 18 of chart A): Place next 31 stitches, including underarm marker, on holder.

Place marker for beginning of steek. Cast on 7 sts on right needle using the backward loop method (see page 124). Place marker for end of steek. Join again by knitting into next st on left needle.

Knit to 15 sts before right underarm marker. Place next 31 sts and underarm marker on holder.

Make second armhole steek just like the first, placing markers on each side of steek sts. Work to end of round—264 sts on needle including steeks. Remember to alternate colors in steeks on every st and every round.

SHAPE ARMHOLES

Decreases for armhole shaping are worked on either side of each armhole steek. Discontinue increases/decreases for chart changes from this point on.

Armhole Decreases
Next Round (round 19 of chart A): K1, ssk, knit to 3 sts before first armhole steek, k2tog, k1, knit steek sts, k1, ssk, knit to 3 sts before second armhole steek, k2tog, k1, knit to end of round. Work these decreases every other round 2 more times. Change to chart B aligning first st over previous chart B pattern. Work these decreases every other round 6 more times (9 times total)—228 sts on needle including steeks. Work in established pattern for one more round.

MAKE NECK STEEK

Next Round (round 1 of chart A): Work in pattern for 53 sts. Place next st (center stitch of front) on holder. Place marker and cast on 7 sts for neck steek. Place another marker and join to resume circular knitting. Keeping pattern as established, work one more round.

SHAPE NECK

Next Round (round 3): Knit to last 3 sts before neck steek, k2tog, k1, knit steek, k1, ssk, knit to end of round. Repeat this decrease every other round 7 more times, then every 3rd round 20 times—178 sts on needle including steeks.

Continue with pattern as established until 2 full repeats of charts A and B have been completed from beginning of neck shaping. Work rounds 1–7 of chart A once more. Place all sts on holder.

STITCHING AND CUTTING

Machine stitch and cut the steeks for the neck and both armholes (see page 129).

SHOULDERS

Reserve 25 sts for each shoulder, front and back. Bind off shoulders together (see three-needle bind-off on page 127). Keep center 57 sts on holder for back neck.

NECKBAND

With smaller 24" (60-cm) needle and color A, begin on right front next to center st and pick up by knitting 66 sts to shoulder, 1 st in shoulder seam, knit 57 back neck sts, decreasing 1 st in middle of back neck, 1 st in shoulder seam, 66 sts down front to center st, knit the center st. Place marker on the needle, join, and beginning with color A, work one round in k2, p2 corrugated ribbing (knit the center st with color A)—191 sts.

Decrease Round: Work to last 2 sts before marker, slip 2tog knitwise, remove marker, k1 in color A, p2sso, replace marker. Repeat this decrease every round, working in colors as follows.

■ 106 Mooskit (Color A)

◦ 524 Poppy (Color B)

× 80 Dark Green (Color C)

◇ 788 Leaf (Color D)

+ 198 Peat (Color E)

· 187 Sunrise (Color F)

− 1160 Scotch Broom (Color G)

Chart A

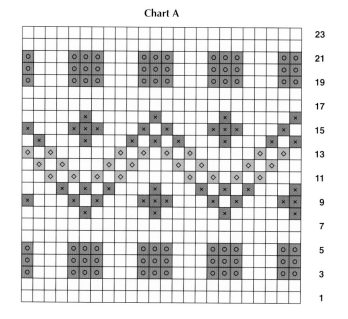

Color Sequence:
Rounds 1–4: *K2 A, p2 B; repeat from *.
Rounds 5–7: *K2 A, p2 C; repeat from *.
Round 8: *K2 A, p2 B; repeat from *.
Round 9: *K2 A, p2 A; repeat from *.
Bind off with A in ribbing.

Chart B

ARMHOLE BANDS

Armhole bands are worked circularly in corrugated ribbing. With smaller 16" (40-cm) needle and color A, begin at middle of underarm and pick up by knitting 160 sts around armhole including underarm sts. Work band color sequence as for neck.

FINISHING

Weave in all ends. Wash and block.

Variations

The vests in this chapter come from various sources of inspiration including other textile traditions, nature, and just basic comfort and good looks.

Wildflowers Waistcoat

The Wildflowers Waistcoat is a personal favorite since it was my first vest design. The pattern was inspired by an embroidered Czechoslovakian wedding dress in the collection of the Museum of International Folk Art in Santa Fe, New Mexico.

Finished Sizes	Chest	Length
Size A	37" (94 cm)	20½" (52 cm)
Size B	40" (101.5 cm)	22" (56 cm)
Size C	43½" (110.5 cm)	23½" (59.5 cm)

Yarn: Cheryl Oberle's Dancing Colors™ Hand-dyed yarn (50% merino/50% mohair, 490 yd [448 m]/ 8 oz hank): Amethyst (Color A), 1 hank; Cha (Color C), 2 oz. Sportweight wool Black (Color B), 600 yd [549 m]

Needles: 24" (60-cm) circular size 3 (3.25 mm) for A, size 4 (3.5 mm) for B, size 5 (3.75 mm) for C. 24" (60-cm) and 16" (40-cm) circular needles two sizes smaller than needle used for body. Adjust needle size if necessary to obtain the correct gauge.

Notions: Four ⅜" (10 mm) buttons; stitch markers; stitch holders

Gauge in two-color pattern on larger needle (see page 128 for swatching techniques)
Size A: 26 sts and 32 rows = 4" (10 cm)
Size B: 24 sts and 30 rows = 4" (10 cm)
Size C: 22 sts and 28 rows = 4" (10 cm)
Remember: Gauge determines how your vest will fit. Swatch until you get it right.

Except for bottom borders, waistcoat is worked circularly to shoulders. Steeks are made for front opening and armholes (see page 129 for steek techniques). Work in St st using the two-color stranding technique (see page 128).

BOTTOM BORDER AND FACING

With smaller 24" (60-cm) needle and black, using a provisional cast-on (see page 124) cast on 232 sts. Work 12 rows St st (knit one row, purl one row), ending with a purl row.

Folding Ridge

Change to larger needle and purl the next RS row. Do not turn work.

STEEK AND JOIN

Place marker and cast on 3 sts onto right needle (needle with yarn attached) using the backward loop method (see page 124). Place marker for end of steek. Join, being sure your sts are not twisted, by knitting into the first st on left needle. This st is the first st of each round.

Knit one round, increasing 2 sts, one on each side of the steek—237 sts including steek.

With black, knit one round placing markers between the 57th and 58th sts and 177th and 178th sts. Knit 4 more rounds.

BEGIN COLOR PATTERN

Work rounds 1–76 of chart once, then work rounds 1–5 once more.

RESERVE UNDERARM STITCHES AND MAKE ARMHOLE STEEKS

Next Round (round 6 of chart): Work to last 4 sts before right side marker, place next 8 sts, including marker, on holder.

Place marker and cast on 3 sts onto right needle (needle with yarn attached) using the backward loop method. Place marker for end of steek. Join again by knitting into first st on left needle.

Knit to 4 sts before left side marker. Make second armhole steek just like the first.

Knit to end of round—227 sts including steeks.

SHAPE ARMHOLE AND NECK

Next Round (round 7 of chart): Knit to 3 sts before right armhole steek, k2tog, k1, knit steek sts, k1, ssk. Knit to 3 sts before left armhole steek, k2tog, k1, knit steek sts, k1, ssk, knit to end.

Repeat armhole shaping every other round 3 more times and **at the same time:** begin neck shaping on round 15 of chart.

Neck Decrease Round: K1, ssk, work to 3 sts before front steek (remember to work armhole decreases), k2tog, k1, knit steek sts.

Repeat armhole shaping 4 more times and neck shaping every other round 9 more times, then every 4th round 7 times—161 sts on needle including steeks.

Continue even until two full repeats of chart have been completed from bottom folding ridge.

■ Amethyst

○ Cha

□ Black

End — Pattern repeat — Begin

SHAPE FRONT SHOULDERS

Shoulders are shaped with short rows as follows (see page 126 for short row techniques):

Set 1: Knit to 8 sts before right armhole steek, wrap next st and turn. Purl to 8 sts before left armhole steek, wrap next st and turn.

Set 2: Knit to 16 sts before right armhole steek, wrap next st and turn. Purl to 16 sts before left armhole steek, wrap next st and turn.

Knit to right armhole steek, hiding wraps.

SHAPE BACK SHOULDERS

Set 1: Knit to 8 sts before left armhole steek, wrap next st and turn. Purl to 8 sts before right armhole steek, wrap next st and turn.

Set 2: Knit to 16 sts before left armhole steek, wrap next st and turn. Purl to 16 sts before right armhole steek, wrap next st and turn.

Knit to end of round, hiding wraps. Place all sts on holder.

STITCH AND CUT

Machine stitch and cut steeks for front opening and armholes (see page 129).

SHOULDERS

Reserve 27 sts for each shoulder, front and back. Keeping the center 44 sts on holder for back neck, bind off shoulders together (see 3-needle bind-off on page 127).

FRONT BANDS

Place safety pins on each side at beginning of V-neck shaping. With smaller 24" (60-cm) needle, black yarn, and beginning at right-front folding ridge, pick up by knitting 64 sts to safety pin, 48 sts to shoulder, 1 st in shoulder seam, 44 back neck sts, 1 st in shoulder seam, 48 sts to next safety pin, and 64 sts to bottom of left front—270 sts. Turn and purl one row. Work 4 rows St st, ending with a purl row.

Buttonholes

Row 1: Knit 4, k2tog, (yo) twice, *k16, k2tog, (yo) twice; repeat from * two more times, knit to end.

Row 2: Purl, working double yarnovers as one st (drop extra loop of double yarnover).

Work 4 rows St st, ending with a purl row.

Folding Ridge

Purl the next RS row.

Border Facing

Beginning and ending with a purl row, work 5 rows St st. Work facing buttonholes as for band.

Work 7 rows St st. Place sts on holder.

Fold border along folding ridge and tack live stitches to inside, covering cut edge of steek. Be sure that the buttonholes line up.

ARMHOLE BANDS

Armhole bands are worked circularly in St st with a facing. With smaller 16" (40-cm) needle, pick up and knit 100 sts around armhole. Join and knit 6 rounds.

Folding Ridge

Purl one round.

Facing

Knit 7 rounds. Place sts on holder. Fold facing along folding ridge and tack live stitches to inside, covering cut edge of steek.

FINISHING

Bottom Facing

Remove provisional cast-on and tack live stitches to inside. Weave in all ends. Wash and block. Sew buttons opposite buttonholes.

Simply Garter

The Simply Garter Vest is just that—a very simple vest worked in garter stitch. The vest is knitted in one piece so there is very little finishing to be done. The lapels can be tacked down at the bottom or left free to be crossed in front. Just remember to cast on loosely to allow the garter-stitch fabric freedom of movement at the bottom of the vest. The vest fits a wide range of sizes due to the wonderful drape and flow of the garter stitch.

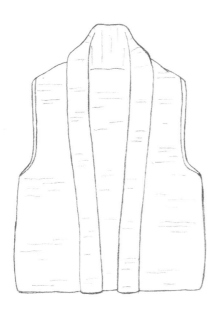

Finished Sizes	Chest	Length
Size A	40–42" (102–107 cm)	20" (51 cm)
Size B	46–48" (117–122 cm)	22½" (57 cm)

Yarn: Cheryl Oberle's Dancing Colors™ (50% merino/50% mohair, 490 yd [448 m]/8oz [227 g]) Bluebonnet, 2 hanks.

Needles: 24" (60-cm) circular size 7 (4.5 mm). 16" (40-cm) circular two sizes smaller than needle used for body.

Notions: Stitch markers; stitch holders

Gauge in garter stitch on larger needle
14 sts and 26 rows = 4" (10 cm)
Stretch the swatch a bit to measure the gauge since the weight of the finished garment will cause the gauge to expand.

Note: Place a marker on the right side of the garment to identify it.

BACK AND FRONTS
Vest is worked in one piece to underarm, then fronts and back are worked separately to shoulders.

With 24" (60-cm) needle and using a long-tail cast-on (or any flexible cast-on) cast on 166 (188) sts. Place marker between the 48th (53rd) and 49th (54th) sts and between the 118th (135th) and 119th (136th) sts. Work in garter st until piece measures 10½ (12½)" (27 [32] cm) from cast-on edge, ending with a WS row.

DIVIDE FOR UNDERARMS/RESERVE UNDERARMS AND FRONTS
Next Row (RS): Knit to 4 (6) sts past first marker and place last 8 (12) sts on holder for right

underarm; knit to 4 (6) sts past second marker and place last 8 (12) sts on holder for left underarm, knit 44 (47). Break off yarn and place both fronts on holders, leaving only the center 62 (70) sts on needle. Knit one more (WS) row.

BACK

Shape Armholes

Next Row (RS): K1, ssk, knit to last 3 sts, k2tog, k1. Repeat this shaping every other row 6 (8) more times (7 [9] times total)—48 (52) sts on needle. Work in pattern until armhole measures 9 (9½)" (23 [24] cm) from underarm, ending with a WS row.

Shape Shoulders

Shoulders are shaped with short rows as follows. (See page 126 for short-row techniques.)

Set 1: *Knit to last 4 (4) sts, slip and wrap next st, turn and repeat from *. Turn.

Set 2: Knit to last 7 (8) sts, slip and wrap next st, turn and repeat from *. Turn.

Set 3: Knit to last 11 (12) sts, slip and wrap next st, turn and repeat from *. Turn and knit to end. Knit one more row, hiding the wraps. Place the 11 (12) sts for each shoulder and the center 26 (28) sts on separate holders.

LEFT FRONT

Place left-front sts on needle. Attach yarn at neck edge and work one WS row.

Shape Armhole

Next Row (RS): K1, ssk, knit to end. Repeat this shaping every other row 6 (8) more times (7 [9] times total)—37 (38) sts on needle. Work in pattern until armhole measures 9 (9½)" (23 [24] cm) from underarm, ending with a RS row.

Shape Shoulder

Set 1: Work to last 4 (4) sts, wrap and turn, work (a RS Row) to end.

Set 2: Work to last 7 (8) sts, wrap and turn, work (a RS Row) to end.

Set 3: Work to last 11 (12) sts, wrap and turn, work (a RS Row) to end.

Knit one more row, hiding wraps. Place the 11 (12) shoulder sts and the 26 lapel sts on separate holders.

RIGHT FRONT

Place right-front sts on needle. Attach yarn at armhole edge and work one WS row.

Shape Armhole

Next Row (RS): Work in pattern to last 3 sts, k2tog, k1. Repeat this shaping every other row 6 (8) more times (7 [9] times total)—37 (38) sts on needle. Work in pattern until armhole measures 9 (9½)" (23 [24] cm) from underarm, ending with a WS row.

Shape Shoulder

Set 1: Work to last 4 (4) sts, wrap and turn, work (a WS Row) to end.

Set 2: Work to last 7 (8) sts, wrap and turn, work (a WS Row) to end.

Set 3: Work to last 11 (12) sts, wrap and turn, work (a WS Row) to end.

Knit 2 more rows, hiding wraps. Place the 11 (12) shoulder sts and the 26 lapel sts on separate holders.

SHOULDERS

With wrong sides held together, bind off shoulders together (see three-needle bind-off on page 127).

COLLAR/LAPELS

Left side

Place 26 lapel sts on needle. Attach yarn at the inner edge and beginning with a RS row, knit one row. Turn.

Row 1: Knit to last st, ssk this st with one from the back neck holder.

Row 2: Knit.

Repeat these 2 rows 12 (13) more times (13[14] times total). Place sts on holder.

Right Side

Place 26 lapel sts on needle. Attach yarn at outer edge and beginning with a RS row work as follows.

Row 1: Knit to last st, ssk this st with one from the back neck holder.

Row 2: Knit.

Repeat these 2 rows 12 (13) more times (13[14] times total). Place sts on holder.

Using garter-stitch grafting (see page 124), graft collar together at center back neck. Turn back lapels and (optional) tack outer corners of lapel down to bottom of body.

ARMHOLE BORDERS

Armhole borders are worked circularly. With 16" (40-cm) needle and beginning at middle of underarm holder, pick up by knitting 90 (94) sts around armhole including underarm sts. Join and purl one round. Knit next round then bind off in purl.

FINISHING

Weave in all ends. Wash and block.

Basic Black

The basic black vest is based on the black waist-coats that are part of daily dress in cultures around the world. A classic shape, this vest would be great in any color.

Finished Sizes	**Chest**	**Length**
Size A	40" (102 cm)	24½" (62 cm)
Size B	44" (112 cm)	25½" (65 cm)
Size C	48" (122 cm)	26½" (67 cm)

Yarn: WoolPak 8 ply (100% wool, 510 yd [466 m]/ 250 g [9 oz]): Black, 2 skeins

Needles: 24" (60-cm) circular size 5 (3.75 mm). 24" (60-cm) and 16" (40-cm) circular needles two sizes smaller than needle used for body. Adjust needle size if necessary to obtain the correct gauge.

Notions: Five ½" (12 mm) buttons; two safety pins; stitch markers; stitch holders; scrap yarn

Gauge in Stockinette stitch on larger needle
20 stitches and 26 rows = 4" (10 cm)
Remember: Gauge determines how your garment will fit. Swatch until you get it right.

Note: Vest is worked in one piece to underarm, then the fronts and back are worked separately to the shoulders.

BACK AND FRONTS
Bottom Facing
With smaller 24" (60-cm) needle and using a provisional cast on (see page 124), cast on 195 (215, 235) sts. Place marker between 48th (52nd, 57th) and 49th (53rd, 58th) sts and between 147th (163rd, 178th) and 148th (164th, 179th) sts. Work 12 rows of St st (knit one row, purl one row) ending with a purl row.

Folding Ridge
Change to larger 24" (60-cm) needle and purl next (RS) row.
Work in St st until piece measures 6 (6, 7)" (15 [15, 18] cm) from folding ridge.

RESERVE POCKET OPENING
Next Row (RS): Knit 10 (11, 13); with contrasting scrap yarn knit the next 20 sts. Turn and knit the same sts again with the scrap yarn. Turn, and with vest yarn, knit 20 pocket sts again. Knit to the last 30 (31, 33) sts, work second pocket opening as first over next 20 sts, knit 10 (11, 13).
Continue in St st until piece measures 14 (14½, 15)" (36 [37, 38] cm) from folding ridge, ending with a purl row.

DIVIDE FOR UNDERARMS/RESERVE UNDERARM AND FRONT STITCHES
Next Row (RS): Knit to 5 (8, 10) sts past first marker; place last 10 (16, 20) sts worked (including marker) on holder for right underarm. Work to 5 (8, 10) sts past second marker and place last 10 (16, 20) sts worked (including marker) on holder for left underarm. Work to end of row, break off yarn, and place both fronts on holders, leaving only center 89 (95, 101) sts on needle for back. With WS facing, join yarn and work one row.

Set 3: On next (RS) row *work to last 12 sts, slip and wrap next st, turn and repeat from * once. Turn.

Next Row (RS): Knit, hiding wraps. Place sts on holder.

LEFT FRONT

Armhole and neck shaping are worked at the same time. Place left-front sts on needle. With WS facing, join yarn at neck edge and work one row.

Next Row (RS): K1, ssk (armhole shaping), knit to last 3 sts, k2tog, k1 (neck shaping). Repeat armhole shaping every other row 11 more times (12 times total) and repeat neck shaping every 4th row 12 (13, 16) more times and then every 6th row 2 times. End on RS row—16 (16, 16) sts on needle.

Shape Shoulder

Set 1: On next (WS) row work to last 4 sts, slip and wrap next st, turn and work to end.

Set 2: On next (WS) row work to last 8 sts, slip and wrap next st, turn and work to end.

Set 3: On next (WS) row work to last 12 sts, slip and wrap next st, turn and work to end.

Next Row (WS): Purl, hiding wraps. Place sts on holder.

RIGHT FRONT

Armhole and neck shaping are worked at the same time. Place right-front sts on needle. With WS facing, join yarn at armhole edge and work one row.

Next Row (RS): K1, ssk (neck shaping), knit to last 3 sts, k2tog, k1 (armhole shaping). Repeat armhole shaping every other row 11 more times (12 times total) and repeat neck shaping every 4th row 12 (13, 16) more times and then every 6th row 2 times. End on RS row—16 (16, 16) sts on needle. Work one WS row.

BACK

Shape Armholes

Next Row (RS): Decrease 1 st at each armhole edge as follows: K1, ssk, work to last 3 sts, k2tog, k1. Repeat this shaping every other row 11 more times (12 times total). Work even until armhole measures 9½ (10, 10½)" (24 [25.5, 27] cm) from the underarm, ending with a WS row.

Shape Shoulders

Shoulders are shaped with short rows as follows (see page 126 for short row techniques):

Set 1: On next (RS) row *work to last 4 sts, slip and wrap next st, turn and repeat from * once. Turn.

Set 2: On next (RS) row *work to last 8 sts, slip and wrap next st, turn and repeat from * once. Turn.

Shape Shoulder
Set 1: On next (RS) row work to last 4 sts, slip and
    wrap next st, turn and work to end.
Set 2: On next (RS) row work to last 8 sts, slip and
    wrap next st, turn and work to end.
Set 3: On next (RS) row work to last 12 sts, slip and
    wrap next st, turn and work to end.
Next Row (RS): Knit, hiding wraps. Place sts on
    holder.

SHOULDERS
Bind off shoulders together (see three-needle bind-off
on page 127).

FRONT AND NECKBANDS
Front and neckbands are worked in one piece in St st
with a facing.

Place safety pins at beginning of V-neck shaping
on each front. With smaller 24" (60-cm) needle and
beginning at bottom right front folding ridge, pick up
by knitting 62 (62, 64) sts to safety pin, 54 (57, 60) to
shoulder, 33 (39, 45) from back neck, 54 (57, 60) to
next safety pin, and 62 (62, 64) sts from pin to bottom
of left front—265 (277, 293) sts on needle. Beginning
with a purl row, work in St st for 3 rows.

Buttonholes (Men's version)
Next Row (RS): Knit 205 (217, 232) (yo) twice, ssk,
    *k12, (yo) twice, ssk, repeat from * 3 more times
    end k2 (2, 3).
Next Row: Purl, working double yarnovers as one
    stitch (drop extra loop of double yarnover).

Work 3 more rows of St st.

Folding Ridge
Knit the next (WS) row.

Border Facing
Starting with a knit row, work 3 more rows of St st, ending with a knit row.

Buttonholes in Facing
Next Row (WS): Purl 2 (2, 3), p2tog, (yo) twice,
    *p12, p2tog, (yo) twice; repeat from * 3 more
    times, purl to end.
Next Row: Knit, working double yarnovers as one
    stitch (drop extra loop of double yarnover).
Work 3 more rows of St st.
    Place sts on holder. Fold facing to WS at folding
ridge and tack down live sts to inside. Be sure to match
up buttonholes.

Buttonholes (Women's version)
Next Row (RS): Knit 2 (2, 3), k2tog, (yo) twice, *k12,
    k2tog, (yo) twice; repeat from * 3 more times,
    knit to end.
Next row: Purl, working double yarn overs as one
    stitch (drop extra loop of double yarn over).
Work 3 more rows of St st.

Folding Ridge
Knit the next (WS) row.

Border Facing
Starting with a knit row, work 3 more rows of St st, end-
ing with a knit row.
Buttonholes in Facing
Next Row (WS): Purl 205 (217, 232), (yo) twice,
    p2tog, *p 12, (yo) twice, p2tog, repeat from * 3
    more times end p2 (2, 3).
Next Row: Knit, working double yarnovers as one
    stitch (drop extra loop of double yarnover).
    Work 3 more rows of St st. Place sts on holder.

Fold facing to WS at folding ridge and tack down live sts to inside. Be sure to match up buttonholes.

ARMHOLE BANDS

Armhole bands are worked circularly in St st with a facing. With 16" (40-cm) needle and beginning at middle of underarm holder, pick up by knitting 107 (119, 127) sts around armhole including underarm sts. Join and knit 2 rounds. Purl next round for folding ridge. Knit 8 more rounds and place sts on holder. Fold facing to WS at folding ridge and tack down live sts to inside.

POCKETS

Pouch pockets are knitted in St st. Keep right side the same as for body. This will make inside of pockets smooth.

Remove scrap yarn from pocket opening. Place 20 top sts on holder. With smaller needle, pick up 20 bottom sts. Beginning with a WS row, attach yarn and purl one row.

Folding Ridge

Knit the next 3 rows.

Continue in St st until flap measures 3" (7.5 cm). Place sts on holder. With smaller needle, pick up the top sts and work in St st for 3" (7.5 cm). Join pocket flaps at bottom, right sides together, with three-needle bind off (see page 127). Sew sides of pockets together.

FINISHING

Bottom Facing

Remove provisional cast-on and tack down live sts to inside. Weave in all ends. Wash and block.

Sew buttons opposite buttonholes.

Cottonwood

The highly textured bark of the cottonwood tree is the inspiration for this vest design. Native to the plains of the United States, cottonwoods once grew in long groves on the banks of great rivers such as the Platte and the Arkansas. Cottonwoods offered many comforts for people living in the often harsh environment: refreshing shade on scorching summer days, shelter from the wind during storms, and firewood for heat and cooking.

Indians of the plains and southwest still use hollowed-out cottonwood trunks to make ceremonial drums, some of which are large enough for many drummers. Some Native Americans believed that each great cottonwood had a spirit and intelligence and could be asked to give help with human affairs.

The Cottonwood Vest is created with a wonderful technique that is a combination of stranded two-color knitting and cable knitting. Worked simply as two-color stranded stripes that are crossed every eighth round, the resulting two-color cables are striking.

The Cottonwood Vest is knitted with only two colors in each row. Using the black background and the hand-painted yarn, the vest is knitted following the pattern chart. The vest is knitted circularly with steeks for the center front, neck, and armholes.

This pattern includes directions for three sizes. There are also two armhole options: the first armhole (A) is deeper to allow the vest to be worn over sweaters and the second armhole (B) is a standard fitted armhole. See page 128 for two-color stranded knitting and steeking techniques and page 125 for hand-washing instructions.

The size of the vest is determined by needle size; a larger garment is made by using a larger needle. For this reason, doing a gauge swatch is very important.

Finished Sizes (zipped, including borders)	Chest	Length
Size A	41½" (105.5 cm)	21½" (54.5 cm)
Size B	44½" (113 cm)	23" (58.5 cm)
Size C	48¼" (122.5 cm)	25" (63.5 cm)

Yarn: Cheryl Oberle's Dancing Colors™ Hand-dyed yarn (50% merino/50% mohair, 490 yd [448 m]/ 8-oz): Ruby, 1 hank; sportweight wool (600 yd [549 m]: Black

Needles: 24" (60-cm) circular size 7 (4.5 mm) for A, size 8 (5 mm) for B, size 9 (5.5 mm) for C. 24"

(60-cm) and 16" (40-cm) circular needles four sizes smaller than needle used for body. Adjust needle size if necessary to obtain the correct gauge.

Notions: One 22–24" separating zipper, black (too long is better than too short as the zipper can be shortened); sewing needle; sewing thread to match zipper; cable needle; stitch markers; stitch holders

Gauge in pattern stitch on larger needle (see page 128 for swatching instructions).
Size A: 28 stitches and 27 rows = 4" (10 cm)
Size B: 26 stitches and 25 rows = 4" (10 cm)
Size C: 24 stitches and 23 rows = 4" (10 cm)
Remember: Gauge determines how your vest will fit. Swatch until you get it right.

Notes: Except for the bottom border facing, the vest is worked circularly up to the shoulders. Steeks are made for the front opening and the armholes (see page 129 for an explanation of steeks). Work cable pattern using the two-color stranding technique (see page 128).

Bottom Border and Facing
The border is worked in St st with a facing. The facing is worked flat and, once completed, the sts are joined with a steek to begin circular knitting.

With smaller 24" (60-cm) needle, black, and using a provisional cast-on (see page 124), cast on 262 sts.

Work 12 rows of St st (knit one row, purl one row) ending with a purl row.

Folding Ridge
Change to larger 24" (60-cm) needle and purl the next (RS) row. *Do not turn.*

STEEK AND JOIN
Place marker for beginning of steek. Make steek by casting 5 sts onto the right needle (needle with yarn attached) using the backward loop method (see page 124). Place marker for end of steek. When knitting steeks, alternate colors on every st and every round.

Being careful not to twist sts, join into a round by knitting into the first st on left needle. This st is the first st of each round.

With black, knit the first round, increasing 20 sts as follows; knit 7, inc 1, *knit 13, inc 1, repeat from * to last 13 sts, knit to end of round—287 sts on needle. Place marker between the 70th and 71st sts and between the 212th and 213th sts. There are 70 sts on each front and 142 sts on back (counted between steek and underarm markers for fronts and between underarm markers for back).

MAIN COLOR PATTERN
4/4 Left Cross: Place 2 black and 2 color sts on cn and hold in front, knit next 2 black and 2 color sts, knit 2 black and 2 color sts from cn.

Begin chart and work 9 repeats of rounds 1–8 (72 rounds total). (For armhole B, work 10 repeats of rounds 1–8 [80 rounds total], then complete as written.)

RESERVE UNDERARM STITCHES
Next Round: Work to 17 sts before first underarm marker. Place next 36 sts, including underarm marker, on holder.

MAKE ARMHOLE STEEKS
Place marker for beginning of steek. Cast on 5 sts on right needle using the backward loop method. Place marker for end of steek. Join again by knitting into next st on left needle.

Knit to 19 sts before second underarm marker. Place next 36 sts, including underarm marker, on holder.

Make second armhole steek just like the first, placing markers on each side of steek sts.

Knit to end of round—225 sts on needle including steek sts.

SHAPE ARMHOLES

Decreases for armhole shaping are worked on either side of each armhole steek. Remember to alternate colors on steek stitches.

Armhole Decreases

Next Round: Knit to 3 sts before first armhole steek, k2tog, k1, knit steek sts, k1, ssk. Knit to 3 sts before second armhole steek, k2tog, k1, knit steek sts, k1, ssk, knit to end of round. Work these decreases every other round 5 more times (6 times total)—201 sts on needle including steeks.

Work in established pattern until 14 full repeats of rounds 1–8 of chart have been completed, then work rounds 1–5 once more (118 rounds total from beginning). Break off yarns.

RESERVE NECK STITCHES AND MAKE NECK STEEK

Place center 49 sts (22 sts on each side of center steek and center steek sts) on holder.

Next Round (round 6 of chart): At right front, reattach yarns and, keeping pattern as established, complete round in pattern. At end of round, pm on right needle and cast on 5 sts for neck steek. Place another marker on right needle and join to resume circular knitting. Keeping in pattern as established, work one more round (round 7)—157 sts on needle including steeks.

Place 2 black and 2 color sts on cn and hold in front, knit next 2 black and 2 color sts, knit 2 black and 2 color sts from cn.

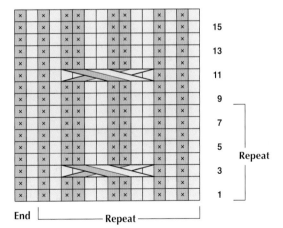

SHAPE NECK

Next Round (round 8): Decrease 1 st at each side of neck steek as follows: k1, ssk, knit to 3 sts before neck steek, k2tog, k1. Repeat this decrease every other round 2 more times—151 sts on needle including steeks.

Continue in pattern as established until 18 full repeats of rounds 1–8 of chart have been completed (145 rounds total from folding ridge). Place all sts on holder.

STITCHING AND CUTTING

Machine stitch and cut the steek for the front opening, the neck, and both armholes (see page 129).

SHOULDERS

Reserve 22 sts for each shoulder, front and back. Bind off shoulders together (see three-needle bind-off on page 127). Keep center 48 sts on holder for back neck.

FRONT BANDS

Bands are knit in St st and roll toward the vest body.

Right Front

With smaller 24" (60-cm) needle and black, begin at right front folding ridge and pick up by knitting 80 sts along right front edge. Beginning with a purl row, work in St st for 13 rows. Bind off loosely.

Left Front

With smaller 24" (60-cm) needle and black, begin at top of the left front, pick up by knitting 80 sts along left front to folding ridge. Beginning with a purl row, work in St st for 13 rows. Bind off loosely.

NECKBAND

With smaller 24" (60-cm) needle and black and beginning at top of right-front band, pick up by knitting 134 sts around neck edge as follows: pick up 3 sts across rolled top edge of right-front band, 22 sts from right-front neck holder, 18 sts to shoulder, 48 sts from back neck holder, 18 sts from shoulder to left-front neck holder, 22 sts from that holder, and 3 sts across rolled top edge of left-front band. Beginning with a purl row and decreasing 1 st (p2tog) above each cable on fronts and back (8 decreases—126 sts on needle), work in St st for 13 rows. Bind off loosely.

ARMHOLE BANDS

Bands are worked circularly in St st and roll toward right side of vest.

With smaller 16" (40-cm) needle and black, begin at middle of underarm and pick up by knitting 128 stitches (116 for Armhole B) around armhole including underarm sts. Join and knit 13 rounds. Bind off loosely.

FINISHING

Bottom Facing

Remove provisional cast-on and tack down live sts to inside. Weave in all ends. Wash and block.

Sew in zipper (see page 121).

ZIPPER (PERDIE'S ZIPPER TECHNIQUE)

First Half: Turn garment inside out. Starting at the bottom and with zipper closed, pin zipper in place on right front only, making sure that bottom of zipper starts at the bottom of garment. Open zipper and remove the other half. Thread sewing needle with single thread. Tack down bottom of zipper tape securely with matching thread. **Note:** The stiff plastic tab at the bottom of the zipper can make this step difficult. Use a thimble to push the needle through the plastic tab. Working from bottom to top, use a small backstitch through the middle of the tape to sew zipper tape to garment, making sure that the zipper stays straight along the edge. No stitches should show on the right side. Stop about an inch from the top. Shorten zipper length if necessary by making a new stop with a bar tack through the zipper teeth at desired stopping point. With sharp scissors, carefully snip through zipper teeth above new bar tack stop and trim away from tape leaving tape attached. Do not cut off tape but cut it at an angle after removing excess teeth. *Hint:* Count the number of teeth cut off so that the same number can be removed on the second half. Tuck tape under, finish stitching up to top, and tack down even with the top of the garment. To finish, tack the edge of the zipper tape down to garment.

Second Half: Zip on other half of zipper and pin into place to match first side. Open zipper and, beginning at the top, shorten zipper as on first side, tack down top edge, and stitch into place as for first side. Whip stitch edge of tape to garment to finish.

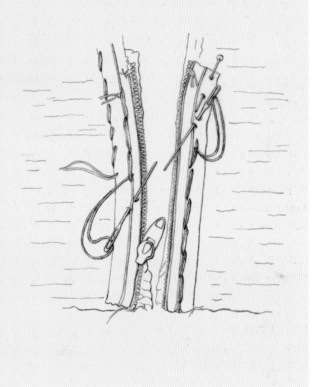

14

Materials and Techniques

MATERIALS

BUTTONS

Unless you are positive that the buttons you have chosen for your vest are washable, sew them on *after* washing and blocking the garment. Special button pins, available in most fabric stores, will work to attach buttons that you do not want to wash.

STITCH HOLDERS

Try using contrasting color scrap yarn or lightweight cotton string to hold stitches. On circular garments in particular, the stitching and cutting is much easier if the stitches aren't all bunched up on a rigid metal holder. Use a finishing needle threaded with scrap yarn and slip the stitches to be held onto the yarn. Be generous and give yourself lots of yarn for each holder. Tie the scrap yarn so that the stitches can't slip off. When picking up the stitches from the holder, leave the holder in until you are sure that all the stitches are on the needle and you are happily knitting along again.

SUBSTITUTING YARNS

So many yarns, so little time! The sources for the yarns used in this book are listed on page 132. If you decide to try a different yarn than is called for in the patterns, you can do so successfully by following these guidelines.

1) Choose a yarn with the same gauge as the yarn used in the pattern; a different weight yarn will

have a different stitch gauge and your garment will have a dramatically different fit.

2) Buy the amount of yardage specified in the pattern. Your local yarn shop can be most helpful here as they have a book that lists the weight and yardage of hundreds of yarns and can make sure that you get enough of your substitute yarn to finish the project. The ball bands of most yarns provide this information as well. To determine the yardage you need, multiply the number of yards per ball for the original yarn by the number of balls required. Then divide this sum by the yards per ball for the substitute yarn; the result will be the number of balls you need of the substitute yarn.

3) If the yarn you have purchased has a different color, fiber content and/or texture, please do a swatch before deciding to use the yarn; it may not behave or look the way you would expect just from seeing it in the ball.

TECHNIQUES

CASTING ON

Long-tail cast-on Leaving a long tail (three to four times the length of the finished piece) make a slip knot and place it on the needle. Place the thumb and index finger of your left hand between the two strands from top to bottom, making sure that the tail is over your thumb and the working yarn is over your index finger. Secure the strands with your other three fingers. Twist your wrist up so that your palm faces upward, and spread your thumb and index finger apart to make a V of the yarn.

Insert the needle into the yarn around your thumb from front to back. Place the needle over the yarn around your index finger and bring the needle down through the loop around your thumb. Drop the loop off your thumb and, returning to the V position, tighten the resulting stitch on the needle. Repeat this process until all the stitches are cast on.

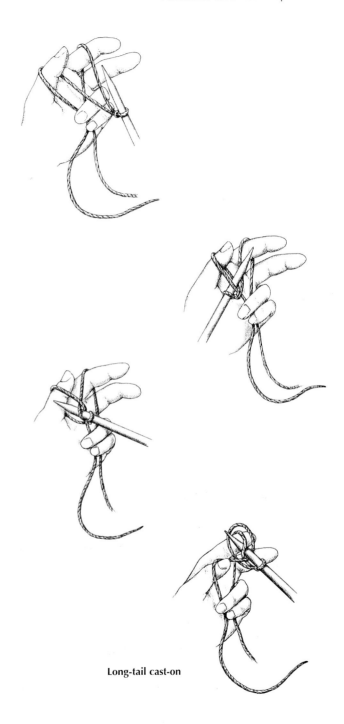

Long-tail cast-on

Backward loop cast-on Twist the yarn into a loop and place the loop on the right needle. Repeat for desired number of stitches.

Provisional cast-on There are many ways to cast on provisionally. I like the crochet-over-the-needle method because it is easy to start and comes out quickly.

With contrasting scrap yarn, make a slip knot and place it on a crochet hook. Hold the yarn in your left hand and the hook in your right. Hold a needle on top of the long strand of yarn in your left hand. *With hook, draw a loop over the needle and through the slip knot (Figure 1). You will now have pulled the yarn over the knitting needle and cast on a stitch. Place the yarn behind the knitting needle (Figure 2) and repeat from * until you have the required number of stitches on the needle. With the last loop still on the crochet hook, cut the yarn and slip the tail through the loop on the hook. Pull up loosely. When you're ready to take out the cast-on, pull the tail out of the last loop and tug on it to unchain the cast-on edge and place the stitches on a needle.

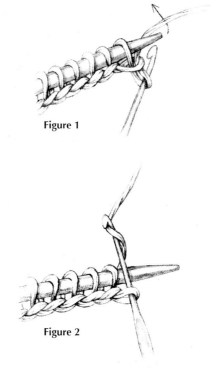

Figure 1

Figure 2

CHART READING

Each square on the chart represents a stitch. The legend for the chart will indicate which symbols stand for which colors and/or stitches. Charts are read from bottom to top. When knitting back and forth, right-side rows are read from right to left and wrong-side rows from left to right. When knitting circularly, all rounds are read from right to left. Enlarge charts on a copying machine, if necessary, to make them easier to read.

A magnetic board will help you keep track of charted patterns. Put the chart on the board and place the magnetic strip directly above the row being worked. Move the magnet up as each row is completed. Post-its work too, and can be used to keep pattern notes as well.

DECREASES

Ssk Slip two stitches individually to right needle knitwise, slip left needle through front of stitches, knit two together through back loops.

K2tog Knit two stitches together.

GARTER-STITCH GRAFTING

For the garter-stitch pattern to be continuous, the front piece must end on a WS row, and the back piece must end on a RS row. Hold the two sets of stitches with right sides up.

Setup: Bring the tapestry needle through the first stitch on the front needle purlwise and leave the stitch on the needle. Bring the tapestry needle through the first stitch on the back needle purlwise and leave that stitch on the needle.

Step 1: Bring the tapestry needle through the same stitch on the front needle knitwise and slip the stitch off the needle. Bring the tapestry needle through the next stitch on the front needle purlwise and leave the stitch on the needle.

Step 2: Bring the tapestry needle through the same stitch on the back needle knitwise and slip the stitch off the needle. Bring the tapestry needle through the next stitch on the back needle purlwise and leave the stitch on the needle.

Repeat Steps 1 and 2 until no stitches remain on the needles, taking care to keep the tension of the grafting yarn the same as that of the knitting.

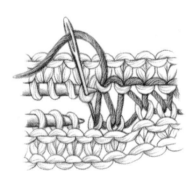

HAND WASHING GUIDE

If you have doubts about washing a particular article, first wash a swatch as a test. Fill a large sink with warm (body temperature) water. Very cold or very hot water "shocks" the fibers, so avoid extremes.

Use a mild soap or your favorite product. I like to use liquid castile soap. Use one or two teaspoons of soap and mix into water with your hand.

Place article to be washed in the water. Gently push it down and squeeze to get it thoroughly wet. Let it soak for ten minutes. Squeeze soapy water through the fabric a few times. Let the water drain out of the sink, pushing the article against the sink to remove most of the soapy water.

Refill the sink with cool water. Gently knead article to rinse out soap. Drain sink again and repeat rinse procedure. If a dye is bleeding excessively, simply continue rinsing until the rinse water is clear. You may add a teaspoon of vinegar to the last rinse to help "set" the dye.

After the last rinse, allow the article to drain well in sink, pushing it against the sides of sink to remove most of the water. Do not wring. Roll the article in a large towel and squeeze so the towel soaks up the excess water or run the article through a washing machine spin cycle. Place the article in the machine and set the cycle selector to a slow spin cycle. Allow machine to spin for two or three minutes and then remove the article and lay it out to dry. A machine-spun article will dry more quickly than a towel-rolled one. If stretching is a concern, as with some cottons, put the article inside a pillowcase before spinning.

Lay out article on a blocking board or on a large towel on the floor and gently smooth out with your hands. Use a tape measure to check the finished measurements. Pin into place if necessary with rustproof pins. Don't stretch too much. Let dry completely.

INCREASES

M1 Increase Twist the yarn into a loop and place it on the right needle. Tighten until snug.

PICKING UP STITCHES BY KNITTING

Holding the garment with right side facing you, insert a needle from front to back and in one stitch from the edge. Wrap the yarn around the needle as if to knit and pull the yarn through, forming a stitch on the needle. Repeat this procedure until the required number of stitches are on the needle.

SHORT ROWS (SLIP AND WRAP)

Knit to the turning point and leave the yarn where it is. *Slip the next stitch as if to purl. Bring yarn to the front (to the back on a purl row) and slip the stitch back to the left needle. Turn. Bring the yarn into the proper position for the next stitch and work back.

To hide the wrap on the knit side, knit it together with the next stitch.

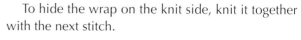

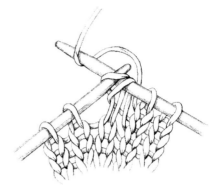

To hide the wrap on the purl side, go into the back of the wrap with the right needle, lift the wrap up onto the left needle, and purl the wrap together with the next stitch.

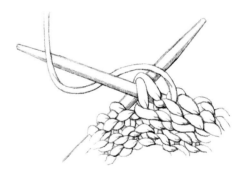

SWATCHING

Swatching is the most important thing that you can do to make sure your garment both looks and fits the way you expect it to. The time you take to knit a swatch will be well spent. By swatching you not only assure that you will get a garment that fits its intended body, but you can also decide if you like the yarn and the pattern and how the fabric will behave when steamed or washed. Your swatch is your best friend! Keep swatching until you get it right.

It's easy to make a swatch. Cast on at least thirty

stitches and work in the stitch pattern specified for the gauge in the pattern. Steam or wash your swatch and allow it to dry. Measure the entire width of the swatch and divide the width into the number of stitches that you have cast on. The resulting number is the number of stitches you are getting per inch. If the pattern states that you need a gauge of twenty-eight stitches to four inches, you need to be getting seven stitches to the inch (twenty-eight stitches divided by four inches). Many of the patterns in this book require only a stockinette-stitch or garter-stitch swatch; the two-color patterns will need to be swatched using the two-color stranding method. Read the section on two-color knitting techniques for detailed two-color swatch instructions.

THREE-NEEDLE BIND-OFF

Place the two sets of stitches to be joined on separate needles. With the right sides together, *hold the needles parallel in your left hand. With a third needle in your right hand, join the yarn and knit together one stitch from each needle (one from the front needle, one from the back needle). Repeat this on the next pair of stitches. You will now have two stitches on the right-hand needle. Pass the first stitch on the right needle over the second stitch as in regular bind off. Repeat the procedure, knitting front and back stitches together and then binding off until all the stitches are bound off.

   *If you want a ridge on the outside, hold wrong sides together.

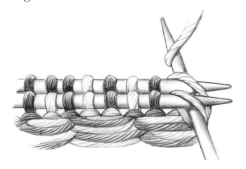

THREE-STITCH I-CORD (KNIT AND ATTACH)

With double-pointed needles, cast on three stitches. *Slide stitches to the other end of the needle. Bringing yarn up across the back from the bottom stitch, knit two stitches, pick up a strand of yarn from the edge of the garment, and ssk it together with the last slipped stitch of the I-cord. Repeat from *.

TWISTED CORD

Cut a length of yarn about six times the length of the cord desired. (Several strands may be used for a heavier cord.) Double the strand of yarn and tie the yarn ends into a knot.

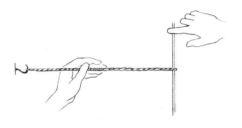

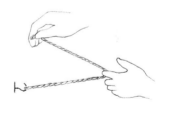

Secure the knotted end on a hook or a doorknob and place a pencil through the looped end. Twist the cord by spinning the pencil around until it is "overspun" or twists back on itself when the cord is slightly slack. Holding the middle of the twisted yarn, bring the yarn ends together. Let the yarn twist back on itself from the middle. Smooth the yarn with your fingers to even out any bumps.

TWO-COLOR KNITTING TECHNIQUES
Swatching

When knitting your swatch, start with the suggested needle for your chosen size and change the needle as necessary to obtain the given gauge for your size garment. To get an accurate gauge measurement for circular two-color knitting, make your swatch as follows. **Note:** When working with two colors in a row, knit the first and last stitches with *both* colors held together to anchor the yarns and produce an even tension.

With one color of yarn and circular needle, cast on thirty-two stitches (thirty pattern stitches plus two anchor stitches). Knit one row. At the end of the row, break off the yarn leaving a three-inch tail. *Do not turn work.* Instead, slide all the stitches to the other end of the needle, join both colors, leaving a three-inch tail, and knit the second row (one anchor stitch with both colors held together, thirty stitches from chart using two-color stranding, and one more anchor stitch with both colors held together). Break yarns, leaving a three-inch tail. Repeat this knitting and sliding, breaking and rejoining the yarns on every row. In this way you are knitting every row (no purling) and simulating the gauge that you will have when you are knitting every row on your circular project.

You may tie the ends of the yarn together on the sides to keep the proper tension. Tie the ends as you knit or wait until the swatch is finished. Do tie them before washing and measuring your swatch.

Wash and block your swatch (see the Hand Wash-ing Guide). When it is dry, measure its entire width between the edge stitches, i.e., do not count the two outside stitches.

Stranding and Catching

When knitting with two colors in each row, carry the yarn not in use loosely across the back of the work. When you are finished with one color, drop it and begin knitting with the other color. To keep the yarns from twisting when carrying them across each other, bring one strand underneath the other and bring the other strand over the top. Make a note of which color goes over and which goes under and be consistent throughout the garment.

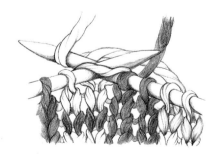

To avoid leaving long carried threads that may catch on buttons or fingers, the yarn must not be carried over more than an inch worth of stitches. If the pattern requires that the yarn be carried over more than an inch, it should be caught in back at least once, more than once for very long strands.

To catch the yarn, simply twist it around the knitting yarn so that it is held in place by the next knitted stitch. The carried yarn will not show through to the front when it is twisted around the knitting yarn correctly. If it is necessary to catch the carried yarn on several consecutive rounds, do not catch it at the same place—knit one more or one less stitch before twisting the yarns. Carried yarns caught on the same stitch on consecutive rows will show through to the front between the knitted stitches.

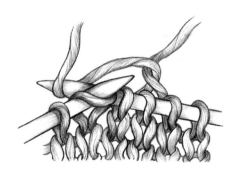

Tension in Two-color Knitting

Always maintain a relaxed tension while stranding and catching the yarn being carried. If the yarn is pulled too tightly across the back of the work, the knitting will draw up and look puckered. To keep the carried yarn at a good tension, spread the stitches on the right needle out on the needle before bringing the carried yarn across the back. This will allow for plenty of slack in the carried yarn and keep the knitted fabric smooth.

STEEKS

A steek consists of a number of extra stitches that will be cut to create an opening in a circularly knit garment. To make a steek, first put stitches on hold if called for in the pattern. On the right needle, cast on required number of stitches (with both strands held together if knitting with two colors) using the backward loop method (see page 124), and continue knitting in the round. Place markers on each side of the steek so that you recognize it when you come to it. When working with two colors in a row, alternate the colors in the steek on every stitch and every row to be sure that each color is secure before cutting.

Shaping Around a Steek

Whether for neckline or for armholes, openings are shaped by working decreases on each side of the steek stitches. Make mirror-image decreases by using k2tog on one side and ssk on the other. Keep a plain knit stitch on each side between the decrease and the steek; the decreases will not fall awkwardly on the very edge of the opening and the plain knit stitch will provide a clean edge from which to later pick up stitches.

Stitching and Cutting

After the body of the sweater is complete, the steeks are stitched on a sewing machine and cut to make the openings. A very wide steek may not require machine stitching. The pattern will indicate the method to use, but if in doubt, always machine stitch.

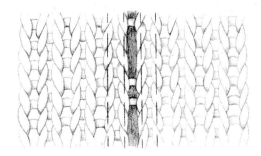

First securely work in the ends of yarn along the edge of the steek. Be sure to close any gap that occurs between the steek and the first stitch of the row. Mark the center stitch of the steek by basting with yarn of a highly contrasting color. Make sure that most of the basting thread shows on the front so you can use it as your stitching guide. Set your sewing machine for a short stitch. Make two rows of machine stitching on each side of the center stitch. As you are stitching, make sure the knitted fabric does not pucker. It is better to stretch the fabric slightly.

After completing all four rows of machine stitching, cut your sweater on the basting line down the center of the steek, between the rows of machine stitching.

STITCH PATTERNS
Garter Stitch
When working circularly, alternately knit a round and purl a round. When working back and forth, knit every row.

Stockinette Stitch
When working circularly, knit every round. When working back and forth, knit the right-side rows and purl the wrong-side rows.

Abbreviations

BO	bind off
cn	cable needle
CO	cast on
k	knit
k1b	knit 1 in back of stitch
k2b	knit 2 in back of next two stitches
k2tog	knit 2 stitches together
m1	make one increase by adding backward loop
p	purl
pm	place marker
p2sso	pass 2 slipped sts over
RS	right side
ssk	slip 2 stitches individually to right needle knitwise, slip left needle through front of stitches, and k2tog through back loops
st(s)	stitch(es)
St st	stockinette stitch
WS	wrong side
yo	yarn over

Acknowledgments

olk Vests was inspired by many hearts and is the work of many hands. To my test knitters, Anne Reed, Lynn Gates, Joan Deneen, Donna Hunt, Jan Cornelius, Joy Stout, Jean Knapp, and the Handknitter's Guild of North Central Texas, all my thanks for your talent, time, and patience. These vests would not have become a reality without you.

My heartfelt gratitude goes to the talented and resourceful Judith Durant and Dot Ratigan, a wonderful team of editors that kept me on track and in line.

Many thanks to the production staff at Interweave Press for their diligent and beautiful work and to Linda Ligon for giving me the opportunity to once again delve into the knitting and folklore of the world.

Thanks also to Joe Coca and Timothy Basgall for their great photos.

For generously supplying yarn, many thanks to Meg Swanson and Schoolhouse Press, Deb Gremlitz and Nordic Fiber Arts, Blackwater Abbey Yarns, Weaving Southwest, La Lana Wools, Rowan Yarns, Himalaya Yarns, Baabajoes, and Unicorn Books and Crafts.

I am grateful as well to Rachel Brown, Barbara Thacker, Anni Kristensen, John Marshall, Nancy Bush, Sasha Kagan, Tony Shaw, and Perdie Woll for sharing their information and inspiration.

Thanks to my mother, Jane Goughnour, for giving me the gifts of knitting and persistence.

And to Gary Oberle, my husband and friend, thanks for your wonderful lino-cuts, and for always believing that I could do this.

Yarn Resources

Baabajoes
Woolpak Yarns
www.baabajoeswool.com

Blackwater Abbey Yarns
1135 S. Dahlia St.
Denver, CO 80246
(303) 756-2714
www.abbeyyarns.com

Cheryl Oberle Designs
3315 Newton St.
Denver, CO 80211
(303) 433-9205
www.cheryloberle.com

Himalaya Yarns
149 Mallad Dr.
Clochester, VT 05446
(802) 658-6274
http://himalaya-yarn.home.att.net

Knit One Crochet Two
Parfait Solids
Ventura, CA 93003
(800) 607-2462

La Lana Wools
136-C Paseo Norte
Taos, NM 87571
(505) 758-9631
www.lalanawools.com

Nordic Fiber Arts
Rauma Strikkegarn
4 Cutts Rd.
Durham, NH 03824
(603) 868-1196
www.nordicfiberarts.com

Reynolds Yarns Inc.
Turnberry Tweed
445 Main St.
West Townsend, MA 01469

Rocky Mountain Llama Fiber Pool
(970) 568-3747
(970) 666-9437

Schoolhouse Press
Québécoise and Jamieson and Smith
6899 Cary Bluff
Pittsville, WI 54466
(800) 968-5648
www.schoolhousepress.com

Unicorn Books and Crafts
Jamieson's 2-ply Shetland
1338 Ross St.
Petaluma, CA 94954
(707) 762-3362
www.unicornbooks.com

Weaving Southwest
216 b Pueblo Norte
Taos, NM 87571
(505) 758-0433
www.weavingsouthwest.com

Westminster Trading
Rowan Yarns
(800) 445-9276

Bibliography

Baer, Joshua. *Collecting the Navajo Child's Blanket.* Santa Fe, New Mexico: Morningstar Gallery, 1986.

Briggs, Katherine. *An Encyclopedia of Fairies.* New York: Pantheon Books, 1976.

Brubriski, Kevin. *Portrait of Nepal.* San Francisco: Chronicle Books, 1993.

Bush, Nancy. *Folk Socks.* Loveland, Colorado: Interweave Press, 1994.

Edain, McCoy. *A Witch's Guide to Faery Folk.* St. Paul, Minnesota: Llewllyn Publications, 1994.

Fanderl, Lisl. *Bauerliches Stricken 2.* Germany: Rosenheimer, 1979.

Frazer, George James. *The New Golden Bough.* Garden City, New York: AnchorBooks Doubleday & Company, Inc., 1961.

Grant, I. F. *Highland Folk Ways.* Edinburgh, Scotland: Birlinn Limited, 1995.

Harmony Guide to Aran Knitting. London: Lyric Books Ltd., 1991.

Harold, Robert, and Phyllida Legg. *Folk Costumes of the World.* London: Blandford, 1978.

Hedrick, Basil C., and Anne K. Hedrick. *Historical and Cultural Dictionary of Nepal.* Metuchen, New Jersey: The Scarecrow Press, 1972.

Jackson, Anna. *Japanese Country Textiles.* New York: Weatherhill, Inc., 1997.

Kahlenberg, Mary Hunt. *The Extraordinary in the Ordinary: Textiles and Objects from the Collections of Lloyd Cotson and the Neutrogena Corporation.* New York: Harry N. Abrams, Inc., 1998.

Katoh, Amy Sylvester. *Japan Country Living.* Tokyo: Charles E. Tuttle, 1993.

Koch, William E. *Folklore from Kansas: Customs, Beliefs, and Superstitions.* Lawrence, Kansas: University Press of Kansas, 1980.

Koren, Leonard. *Wabi-Sabi for Artists, Designers, Poets & Philosophers.* Berkeley, California: Stone Bridge Press, 1994.

Lecount, Cynthia Gravelle. *Andean Folk Knitting: Traditions and Techniques from Peru and Bolivia.* St. Paul, Minnesota: Dos Tejedoras Fiber Arts Publications, 1990.

Marshall, John. *Make Your Own Japanese Clothes.* Tokyo, Japan: Kodansha International, 1988.

Mayer, Anita Luvera. *Clothing from the Hands that Weave.* Loveland, Colorado: Interweave Press, 1984.

Oberle, Cheryl. *Folk Shawls.* Loveland, Colorado: Interweave Press, 2000.

Rossbach, Sarah. *Living Color: Master Lin Yun's Guide to Feng Shui and the Art of Color.* New York: Kodansha America, Inc., 1994.

Seto, T. *Knitting Patterns 500.* Japan: Vogue Nippon, 1989.

——. *Knitting Patterns 1000.* Japan: Vogue Nippon, 1992.

Shaw, C. *Scottish Myths and Customs.* Glasgow: HarperCollins Publishers, 1997.

Starmore, Alice. *Alice Starmore's Book of Fair Isle Knitting.* Newtown, Connecticut: The Taunton Press, 1988.

Sundbo, Annemor. *Everyday Knitting: Treasures from a Ragpile.* Kristiansand, Norway: Torridal Tweed, 2000.

Telesco. Patricia. *Folkways: Reclaiming the Magic and Wisdom.* St. Paul, Minnesota: Llewllyn Publications, 1995.

Thompson, Gladys. *Patterns for Guernseys, Jerseys and Arans.* New York: Dover Publications, Inc., 1979.

Tilke, Max. *Costume Patterns and Designs.* New York: Rizzoli International Publications, Inc., 1990.

Walker, Barbara G. *A Second Treasury of Knitting Patterns.* New York: Charles Schribner's Sons, 1970.

——. *A Treasury of Knitting Patterns.* New York: Charles Schribner's Sons, 1968.

——. *The Women's Dictionary of Symbols and Sacred Objects.* San Francisco: HarperSanFrancisco, 1988.

Index